D1478530

The
Fire of
Creation

The Fire of Creation

BY

J. J. VAN DER LEEUW

Published under a grant from the Kern Foundation

THE THEOSOPHICAL PUBLISHING HOUSE
Wheaton, Ill., U.S.A.
Madras, India/London, England

©Copyright by The Theosophical Publishing
House, Wheaton, Illinois

First Quest edition, 1976, published by the
Theosophical Publishing House, Wheaton,
Illinois, a department of the Theosophical
Society in America

Library of Congress Cataloging in Publication Data

Leeuw, Jacobus Johnnes van der, 1893—
    The fire of creation.

    Reprint of the ed. published by the
    Theosophical Press, Chicago.
    "A Quest book."
    Includes index.
    1. Theosophy.   I. Title.
BP565.L63F57   1976   212'.52   75-26823
ISBN 0-8356-0470-5

Printed in the United States of America

CONTENTS

First Section
The Holy Ghost as the Creator

CHAPTER I

THE HOLY SPIRIT A NEGLECTED CHAPTER IN RELIGIOUS HISTORY

CHAPTER II

THE FIRE OF CREATION

CHAPTER III

THE RHYTHM OF LIFE

CHAPTER IV

THE DIVINE RITUAL

CHAPTER XII

THE LORD OF THE FIVE RAYS

Fourth Section

The Motherhood of God

CHAPTER XIII

THE MOTHERHOOD OF GOD

FOREWORD BY C. JINARĀJADĀSA

"The reign of the Father is past; the reign of the Son is passing; the reign of the Spirit is at hand." So runs the mystic prophecy of Joachim of Flora. It is the theme of this work. I have rarely read a work with whose general argument I concur so heartily as with this striking essay of Dr. J. J. van der Leeuw. What he says concerning the divine Mind and its creative touch in us is a doctrine which I have myself tried to familiarize. "Day-dreaming" has ever been to me an act of creation, truly a "living in the future," but it is only on reading this essay that I realize clearly its relation to the Trinity in man.

There is one proof of the change "from the Son to the Holy Ghost," and it is in the myriads of lines of activity originated by men today. These are the days of associations for reform. Men and women, and especially youth, feel themselves driven from within to go and break down the old world and reconstruct a new. It is noteworthy that, in the carrying out of this inner impulse, the reformer does not especially rely upon any inspiration from "the Father" or from "the Son." The reformer does not turn to religion; he turns to the problem and looks to his enthusiasm for reform to give him the fullest consecration.

The new era of the Holy Ghost with its Fire of Creation is also evidenced by the fact that men and women of every religion now meet together for high religious purposes, but only, if one may speak in paradox, by forgetting their religion. The existing religions which teach men to worship the Father (Hinduism and Islam), or the Son (Christianity), tend to divide rather than to unite the world. I do not say this in any derogatory sense, because each religion is a way to perfection, but none of them is the best among them all. But hitherto, men have been taught to tread along that particular religious path on which their feet have been set at birth, and not to attempt other paths. It was best so for them then, at that epoch of the World-Spirit's self-revelation. But the Day of Brahmā is once more at hand. His creative fire makes men see each other's faces in a new light, and Hindu or Buddhist,

Christian or Moslem, Parsi or Hebrew, become mere labels of a bygone age. Fully characteristic of the coming Day of Brahmā are those movements which stress the reality of the one world, with emphasis upon service rather than upon creeds.

Another evidence of the coming era of the Holy Ghost is that more and more the tendency now is from action to knowledge, not as hitherto from knowledge to action. Those who have been touched by the Fire of Creation plunge into action, trusting to find their religion afterwards. If their action has been motivated by idealism, the coming of their religion is utterly sure. More and more the priest of the new age will not say to his congregation: "Let us pray," but rather: "Let us act." For to act with a right motive is to come to the heart of prayer, and not who "prayeth best" but who *saveth* best will be the saint of the new dispensation. The world has more religion than it needs, more science than it can assimilate; one thing alone is lacking, the fire of enthusiasm. Yet that divine enthusiasm is ready for our possession, if only we will stretch out our hands and grasp. This book will, I feel sure, suggest ways, not of possessing, but of being possessed by the Fire of Creation.

C. JINARĀJADĀSA

PUBLISHER'S NOTE

Dr. van der Leeuw's lucid work on the place and function of the Third Person of the Trinity, the Holy Ghost, in the divine scheme of things is unique in all of theosophical literature. It has been out of print for a number of years; now, in answer to numerous requests, it is once more being made available as a Quest Book in the Theosophical Classics Series. *Fire of Creation* deals with a subject little understood and long neglected or ignored in most of the religions of the world. Its timeless message has special relevance today, in a world floundering in the confusion of kaleidescopic change. Some minor editing has been done to prevent possible misunderstanding and to bring the typography in line with modern usage. A few clarifying footnotes have been added. The language of the author has been retained, however, and his message is precisely as it was given in the original work.

PREFACE

The present book is the outcome of a series of talks given to a group of students interested in the meaning and work of the Third Person of the Divine Trinity, called in the Christian religion God the Holy Ghost. I had hoped to work out the shorthand-reports of these talks into a carefully planned and written book, but the pressure of work has a tendency to increase instead of to lessen, and I found myself faced with the choice of either using these imperfect reports with some slight alterations or else postponing the publication of the book for an indefinite number of years. As I feel it is a matter of urgency that something more should be known about the present subject, I decided in favor of the first of these alternatives.

I strongly feel that the book is unworthy of the great subject with which it deals, and in many parts I have been able only to outline certain doctrines instead of discussing them fully. This is especially true with regard to the chapter on the Holy Ghost as the Divine Mind.

The Divine Trinity as mentioned in this book is not that eternal Trinity of the nameless Reality behind all universes, but that Trinity as manifest in the Logos of a solar system, who, although great beyond all conception, is yet a manifested Being, relative, not absolute.

In the chapters "From Image to Archetype" and "The World of the Divine Mind," the philosophical points there raised have, however, made it inevitable to refer to that World of the Real which is the Absolute, the Reality of all worlds. A certain confusion may thus have been caused between that Absolute World of the Real and the World of the Holy Ghost through which this Reality is experienced.

Throughout the book the Third Person of the Trinity has been designated by the Christian name of God the Holy Ghost, but naturally all that has been said is equally true of the Third Person of the Trinity as found in other religions. Thus wherever the words Holy Ghost are used the word *Brahmā* may be substituted without altering the meaning.

In publishing this book I wish to express my gratitude to those friends who have made the publication possible by taking down the talks in shorthand, typing them out or preparing them for publication, especially to Miss Violet Kathleen Maddox, Mr. Harold Morton, Mr. Byron Casselberry, Mr. David Dear, and Mr. Colin Francis. Without their help I could not have attempted to publish the present book and I can only hope that the result may prove worthy of their labors.

As far as I know this is the first book in our theosophical literature dedicated to the work of God the Holy Spirit and the great representative of this principle on earth, the Mahachohan. May it so stimulate others that it will soon be followed by more and better ones and may it be a help to students in their attempts to understand more of the work of the Holy Ghost and to come in touch with this mighty influence. There seems almost no limit to the benefits we can derive from such closer contact, and it is my sincere hope that an ever-growing number will come to know more of that divine Wisdom and supreme creative energy which has so fitly been called the Lord, the Giver of Life.

Sydney
May, 1925   J. J. VAN DER LEEUW

FIRST SECTION

The Holy Ghost as the Creator

THE HOLY SPIRIT, A NEGLECTED CHAPTER IN RELIGIOUS HISTORY

The doctrine of the Trinity is one of the most profound and illuminating teachings which, under different names and forms, are found in many of the great world religions. Far from being a subject fit only for metaphysical speculation and theological subtlety and foreign to our daily life, the triune manifestation of the one Eternal is the fundamental reality of all existence, and permeates every single manifestation of life and form both in the world surrounding us and in the world of our inner life.

It is the greatness of Theosophy or divine Wisdom that in it the same doctrines, which in the lifeless orthodoxy of outer religion appear to us as intellectual fossils, devoid of vital interest, are experienced as glorious realities of which the theological dogmas are as the outer husks. Whereas the dogmatist can but analyze and classify the shriveled remains of what once were fair flowers of living teaching, the one who has caught the vision is able to enter that inner world of living truth, where he himself can see and admire the growing flowers rooted in the living soil of the spiritual world, where he can inhale their fragrance and watch their radiant beauty, observe in fact the living and growing organism, compared to which the dried-up flower of dogma is as death to life. He can drink and quench his spiritual thirst from the waters of living truth, whereas theology so often does but retain and worship the empty vessels in which once upon a time those living waters of truth were brought to man.

But even among those to whom the divine Trinity is so

much more real than it is to many of the adherents of orthodox religions, there is an almost universal neglect of the
Third Person of the Trinity. They may have an appreciation
of the work of the great ruling department of this world, the
work of the divine Ruler or the First Logos; they may be
conscious of the vital importance of the work of the Second
Logos in the great department of divine Love and Wisdom;
but they are hardly aware of the enormous importance of the
third great department, that of the Third Logos, who in the
Christian religion is called the Holy Spirit and in Hinduism
Brahma. Of them it is true, as of so many followers of the
great world religions which teach the doctrine of the Holy
Trinity, that they would be just as happy if the Holy Trinity
consisted of two Persons instead of three.

NEGLECT OF THE THIRD PERSON IN HINDUISM

With regard to these great religions themselves, the defi-
ciency is even more in evidence. Hinduism, for instance,
recognizing the triune Deity as Shiva, Vishnu, and Brahma,
corresponding to the Father, Son, and Holy Ghost in Christianity, has many millions of worshippers of Shiva and Vishnu, and many thousands of temples dedicated to Them, but
in the whole of that vast country of India there is but one
temple of any importance set aside for the worship of
Brahma, namely in Pushkar, near Ajmir in Rajputana. Apart
from this one temple there are only three subsidiary shrines
to Brahma throughout India, and the actual worship given to
the Third Person in Hinduism is almost negligible in comparison to the vast waves of devotion and daily worship rising
to Shiva and Vishnu.

NEGLECT OF THE THIRD PERSON IN CHRISTIANITY

In Christianity the situation is almost worse. Many Christians have some idea of what they mean when they glorify
God the Father, or adore God the Son, but to how many does
it convey any meaning when they say that they worship God
the Holy Ghost? When we try to look into the consciousness

2

of Christian worshippers when they speak of God the Holy Ghost, we receive but a very vague impression: if there is any idea at all attached to the words they utter, we find confused notions of God the Holy Ghost as the Comforter, though it is not clear who is supposed to be comforted, or how the comforting takes place. Then again we meet with primitive conceptions, in which the Holy Spirit appears as a dove, hovering over our Lord at Baptism, though here again we find no comprehension as to why in particular the dove, which is a very meek and gentle creature, should be a symbol of God the Holy Spirit, of whom the main characteristics are not so much mildness and meekness as an irresistible strength of divine creative energy. And above all, there is no vital connection whatever between these vague conceptions of the Holy Ghost with the daily life of those who pretend to worship Him. In the Greek Church, the Third Person is understood, and worship is always offered to God the Holy Ghost. But in general the churches of Christendom have neglected this aspect of the Trinity.

THE HOLY SPIRIT IN THE EARLY CHURCH

This has not always been so. In the very early days of Christianity the Holy Spirit was a reality in the life of Christians. As long as the Christ lived on earth, he naturally was the center of inspiration to his disciples, and they looked to him for teaching and advice in all matters. Then, before his death, the Christ told his followers that even though he himself was about to depart, he would not leave them comfortless but would ask his Father to give them another Paraclete or helper, namely the Spirit of Truth, the Holy Spirit; and he gave the power of calling upon the Holy Ghost to those on whom he laid his hands, as is still done in the church when Holy Orders are conferred. While the priesthood from the earliest days was thus especially linked to God the Holy Spirit, it was possible for all who made the effort to come into contact with the power of the Holy Ghost, and derive from that power the benefits which are called the gifts of the Holy Spirit, such as prophetic speech, inspired teaching, healing the sick, driving out of unclean spirits, speaking in tongues, and many other similar manifestations.

In the early Church this inspiration of the Holy Ghost from within took the place of that inspiration which during the lifetime of Christ his disciples had received through him. Naturally it was not always easy to distinguish between the genuine manifestations of this great power and the often hysterical excesses which presented themselves as manifestations of the Holy Ghost but were in reality the signs of a disordered and unbalanced soul. Thus already St. Paul found it necessary to warn his congregations against such unbalanced and even false manifestations, which in some of these early churches were fast becoming a source of trouble; and a century later, the so-called heresy of Montanism was once again the result of the supposed manifestation of the Holy Ghost in Montanus and in some of his devoted disciples. All this is evidence of the importance attached in the early church to God the Holy Ghost and of the influence of this principle in the religious life of Christians of that time.

LATIN CHRISTIANITY AND THE FATHERHOOD OF GOD

All this changed as Christianity gradually became more and more centered round the Church of Rome. From the earliest days, the appeal of Christianity to the Latin world had not been so much through the gifts of the Holy Ghost as through the conception of one God who was Father to all men and not only to Roman citizens. No longer was the religious life of the countless millions, who lived under Roman rule, to be determined by privileges of birth or citizenship, but henceforth religious life was open to all men, for all were children of one God, Father to all. The yearning for a universal brotherhood of man, including barbarians as well as Romans, was one of the prominent signs of the times, and a symptom of the worldwide spiritual awakening taking place. The popularity of the Mithraic Mysteries was partly due to this aspiration, and when Christianity came with its worldwide appeal to all men, however humble and however sinful, assuring all of the eternal love of God the Father, and offering to all the possibility of that spiritual regeneration which God the Son had achieved triumphantly and had promised to all men, the response was even greater. But it was the thought of the Fatherhood of God, the one Divine Father loving all His children and having sent His only begotten Son to show them the way to the Light, which became the dominant factor in Latin Christianity.

THE WORSHIP OF GOD THE SON IN MEDIEVAL CHRISTIANITY

Once more the keynote of Christianity changes when it spreads to Western Europe. In medieval Christianity it is neither God the Father nor God the Holy Ghost who inspires the religious life of that deeply devotional period, but it is Jesus the Christ, the Man of Sorrows, bearing in his life the burdens of all mankind and, in divine compassion for a sinful world, pouring out his very life in sacrifice, so that the world may be saved, who becomes the central figure of the Church's life. Thus the Middle ages show us a Christianity in which the figure of the Christ is the main object of that intense devotion and mystical piety, of which the medieval mind was so eminently capable. Never has a more fragrant worship, a more tender compassion and a more intimate unity with the life of the Christ enriched the church than in those days when the great saints and mystics of the Middle Ages, in the fervor of their adoration and the fiery devotion of their consecrated lives, attained to spiritual exaltations, which will ever remain as shining lights in the history of the Christian religion with its many dark pages of ignorant bigotry and persecution.

THE RENAISSANCE AND THE COMING REIGN OF GOD THE HOLY GHOST

Once more Christianity changes when man awakens from the inner life of spiritual certainty and deep devotion to the discovery of an outer world surrounding him, which he, man, can conquer and explore. Man discovers that world without at the cost of the world within, and since those times of the Renaissance and the Reformation, in which the spirit of independent religious life asserted itself and man dared to question and think for himself, religious life became more and more externalized until, during the last century, it had practically ceased to be a factor in man's social and individual life. Yet the Renaissance marked the beginning of and the transition to a new period in Christian history, a period in which the dominant factor was to be God the Holy Ghost. The birth of physical science and the universal expansion of man's mind in creative effort are, if rightly understood, so many symptoms of the reign of God the Holy Ghost.

It is possible to trace many such symptoms of the increasing influence of the Holy Ghost. The theory of evolution, a philosophy like Bergson's, the epoch-making contributions of Einstein, as well as the new art with its attempts to picture movement, and, in general, the more intense realization of the Work of God *in* this world surrounding us, all these and more are signs of the times, marking the Reign of the Holy Ghost.

The Christianity of the immediate future will be a Christianity in which God the Holy Ghost occupies the same important position as, in Latin Christianity, God the Father and, in the Middle Ages, God the Son filled in the life of the Church. Naturally the living Christ himself, who is the very Heart of the Christian religion, will ever remain the supreme reality of the Christian Church; but, just as in those past periods of Christian history the divine Persons of the Holy Trinity predominated in turn, so the coming age will be one in which the Holy Ghost will be the pervading influence. Thus more than ever is it essential that we should have a better understanding of the Third Person of the Trinity, and of the work and influence of this principle in our daily life, not only in the Christian religion but in all world religions, for everywhere this coming influence will be felt.

The time is past in which the Holy Ghost could remain a neglected chapter in religious history, and the time has come when the followers of all religions should gain a deeper understanding of the tremendous work and the most valuable inspiration which the Third Person of the divine Trinity, God the Creator, God the Holy Ghost, can give.

THE FIRE OF CREATION

To many the very thought of understanding anything of the nature of the Deity seems almost sacrilegious. They look upon things divine as taught to man by revelation; which revelation they identify with the dogmas of their particular church, and it never occurs to them that man himself should attempt to investigate these mysteries of the Spirit. Their usual reply to any suggestion along these lines is that man is not meant to know all things; and that if God had meant him to understand, He would certainly have said so in the revelation He gave to the world through the Christ. Now this is not a reasonable view; the very fact that in man there is the yearning to understand higher things makes it possible for him to attain to that understanding, and, even though God and the Trinity are mysteries which no human consciousness can thoroughly understand, it is certainly possible for us to catch a glimpse of the reality embodied in these conceptions.

There is nothing in this universe apart from God. There is not God on one side and the universe on the other; there is not a divine Being above and a world devoid of divinity below, but God is present at every point of the universe a can be approached and experienced at every such point. If there were anything besides God, God would not be the omnipotent final Reality, and, though the Deity is no doubt infinitely greater than the universe which is His creation, yet every part and particle of that universe, from the tiniest atom to the mightiest planet, is essentially, entirely and thoroughly divine. Thus God, and therefore the Trinity which is God, is manifest in the world of nature around us, in the atom, the mineral, the plant and the animal, as well as in ourselves.

THE TRINITY IN MAN

As nothing is nearer to ourselves than our own consciousness, and since our own consciousness is the only thing which we can know directly, it is but natural that our attempt to understand something of the divine Trinity, and especially of the Third Person, should begin in and through our own consciousness.

The study of consciousness is psychology, and all psychology recognizes a threefold function of consciousness, namely will, perception and thought, which three correspond to the three aspects of the Trinity, the Father, the Son, and the Holy Ghost respectively. The God within us is triune as well as the God beyond us, for there is but one God and we ourselves are essentially divine. This threefold manifestation of consciousness is called in theosophical literature the human trinity of *Atma,* the divine will, the "volition" of the psychologist; *Buddhi,* the divine love and understanding, the "perception" of psychology; and *Manas*, the divine mind, or the "thought" of psychological literature. This human trinity is more than representative of the divine Trinity; it is in a very wonderful manner one with it. Thus through the *Atma* we may approach the Father-aspect of God, through Buddhi, Christ the Son, and through *Manas,* God the Holy Ghost.

THE THREEFOLD INSTRUMENT OF THE TEMPORARY SELF

We must not confuse consciousness in its three aspects of will, perception, and thought with the instrument through which the self within manifests. Our physical body, our emotional body, and our thought body make the threefold instrument through which consciousness can manifest itself; volition through our physical body, perception through our emotional body, and thought through our mental body. The three bodies contribute to what we term the "personality" of one particular life, the instrument through which the self behind gathers its experience, by means of which it grows. If we would approach the consciousness within, and through it come to a closer understanding of the Trinity of which it is the expression in man, we must first learn by a process of meditation to disentangle our consciousness from the bodies with which we identify ourselves in daily life. When we think of ourselves, we are always apt to picture ourselves with the particular personal appearance we have at this moment, with the qualities of intellect and emotion which are ours—in fact, with all that belongs to our present personality. It is this self-identification of the soul with the instrument through which it expresses itself, which is the first obstacle to be conquered if we would gain the wider understanding we seek.

In the beginning, it is hardly possible for us to think of ourselves as separate from that which for so many years we have considered to be our true selves—our entire physical being bearing our name, having our face, expressing our faculties and qualities; and when first we try to discard that which is not self and strive to realize our true self as separate from that not-self, it almost seems as if nothing were left. What remains of us after we take away our physical appearance, our desires and passions, our thoughts, opinions and prejudices—in fact all that which is our manifestation in daily life? Apparently nothing and yet, when in meditation, we regularly make the attempt to disentangle ourselves from this temporary instrument which we call our personality, and try to see it as just one of the many hundreds of personalities through which life after life the soul within has gathered experience, there comes a moment when the void, which is left after all that is personal has been taken away, begins to be filled by the consciousness of our true self. It is only when the cup of our being has been emptied of personality, that it can be filled with the wine of our divine Life, and when this Life is first experienced in meditation, it is like the entrance into a new world, no longer one of appearances, of phenomena, but one of consciousness, one in which we are identified with that which we desire to know.

The Three Paths

According to the type, or what in theosophical literature is called the Ray,* of the person making the experiment, this contact with the higher self within will be along the line either of will, of love and understanding, or of creative thought. There are three main paths of inner development, corresponding to the Three Persons of the divine Trinity: the path of will corresponding to the Father, the path of love corresponding to the Son, and the path of thought corresponding to the Holy Spirit. It is this last path in which we are interested now, and disentangling ourselves from the personality of the moment, we must try to reach our higher self through this aspect of the mind, or *Manas*. Through it we can come into touch with that Power of the Holy Spirit which we are trying to experience, and when we do succeed in gaining this touch, the experience is a very wonderful one indeed.

The Experience of the Holy Ghost

Our first sensation is that of touching a spiritual live wire; we receive a shock which vitalizes our entire being; we are thrilled by an energy far greater than anything we have ever before contacted; we are electrified into action. In such a moment we not only feel that we want to do things but we feel that we *can* do things; it seems as though no obstacle is able to withstand that tremendous energy which we now feel within us, it is as if we were charged with the very Power of God Himself. Such indeed is the case; the energy of which we are conscious is the creative energy of God, the power of the Holy Spirit, as manifested through our own divine mind. God the Holy Spirit is God in His creative activity, just as thought in man is the creative power by which human life in all worlds is moulded.

The creative Will in the divine Trinity is the Father; God crucified in His own creation is the Son; but God in His

---

*See Ch. XII.

creative activity, thinking His universe and creating it by the power of that divine Thought, is God the Holy Ghost. It is that energy of God which we touch through the higher mind within us, and when we do experience it we realize that there is but one power, one force, one energy, in the entire universe, and that is the creative energy of God, the power of the Holy Spirit. This is true both of the universe surrounding us and of the world of our own consciousness; all force and energy in nature is a manifestation of the creative power of God the Holy Ghost, just as all force and creative energy within ourselves is a manifestation of that same supreme creative power. The force which maintains the atom, which makes it the vortex of energy that modern science has found it to be, the force which makes the sun an apparently inexhaustible source of life and energy, that which makes man in his own inner life a radiant sun of creative energy, an energy which increases as we draw upon it—all that is the manifestation of God the Holy Ghost, the creative energy of the Deity which we thus experience.

When by a sustained effort of meditation we try to touch the power of God the Holy Ghost through the divine thought within us, which is the expression of this aspect in our own consciousness, it is as if we touched the Fire of Creation itself; for a moment we feel ourselves taken up into that cosmic creative power by which solar systems are evolved from nebulae, by which all forms, all life in every world, are sustained, and by which the universe is maintained. There is no describing the splendor and awe-inspiring power of this creative Fire which sustains the world. Imagine a fiery, whirling vortex in which universes are made and unmade; imagine a myriad cataracts of living fire, each spark of which has power to create and destroy; imagine the entire universe, with all that is in it, all matter, all objects and creatures, as part of that gigantic Fire of Creation, caused by It, maintained by It, and in time destroyed by It; imagine looking for a moment into the laboratory of the universe, the crucible in which worlds are made and unmade, the workshop of God the Holy Ghost where the divine Creator calls worlds and creatures into being; try to contact for an instant the immensity of that cosmic creative thought-energy, and you will realize something of the meaning of God the Holy Ghost in our daily existence.

CREATION NEVER FINISHED

How utterly lifeless and insufficient does the old theological conception now seem to us, which looks upon God the Creator as having made the universe in six days, made the clock and wound it up as it were, and who, having created the world and found it to be good, does not occupy himself with it any more, except for an occasional divine interference. Creation is not an act of God done once upon a time; the universe is not a machine which, when once wound up, will run for a world-period, but creation, as Origen has maintained, is eternal. Here again we realize the tremendous difference when we leave the realm of theology, or speculation about God, for that of Theosophy, or experience of God. When speculating about God in a theological way, we may please our own fancy by imagining God to have made His creation, finished it and left it to its own development; but when for a moment in the contemplation of our inner self we succeed in experiencing something of the Divine, we realize that creation is not an act of God, performed once upon a time and after that not repeated, but that creation is the essence of the Divine, the very being of God, and that we can no more separate creation from God than we can separate the rays of the sun from the sun itself. If it were not for the fact that the Divine can hardly be qualified we might say that the nature of God is to create as the nature of the bird is to sing, as the nature of water is to be wet, and as the nature of fire is to give heat. What we are apt to look upon as God's creation is in truth His very being, His manifestation in creative activity, that which in Theosophy we call the Third Logos, in Hinduism, Brahma, and in Christianity, God the Holy Ghost.

Never for a moment is creation interrupted. It is well said in Hindu philosophy that this universe is God's imagination, that as long as God maintains the image or thought-form which is the universe, so long does it exist, but if for a moment that attention were withdrawn, if the image were released, that same instant this apparently solid universe with all its matter and diversity of creatures would vanish into nothingness. Truly, God the Holy Ghost, far from being a subject fit only for theological speculation and subtlety, is a very great and practical Reality of our daily existence, without which there would be no daily existence. All day long, every second of what we call time, the process of creation is taking place; all the time the Life of God is pouring forth into His creation through God the Holy Ghost, who so fitly is called "The Lord, the Giver of Life". It is that divine creative Mind which we can approach through our own higher mind, and which can produce in us those manifold manifestations which are called the gifts of the Holy Ghost. Once we have realized something of this significance of the work of the Holy Spirit, both in the universe around us and in ourselves, we can never again fail to recognize the vital importance of this Third Aspect of the Deity in our existence; the Holy Ghost has become to us a Reality in daily life.

THE RHYTHM OF LIFE

The process of creation is a limitation of the Divine by Himself, a circumscription of His infinite Presence within His universe, a going forth from the unity of the divine bliss into the manifoldness of divine oblivion. There is naught but God; the atom, the plant, the animal, man himself, all are divine throughout. But in His creation God is oblivious of Himself, and even man does not know himself as God in the earlier stages of his evolution. It is only after many, many lives in matter, in which his attention is turned outward toward the created universe, that man rediscovers the divine Self, which is his true self, and begins to tread the path back to God. Thus the goal of human evolution is unification, or at-onement, with the Divine, the *yoga* of the Hindu and the mystic union of the Christian devotee.

The Divine Breath

All creation is thus twofold, a going forth from unity in the Divine to the manifoldness of created existence, and a return from the oblivion in matter to conscious union in God. It is the eternal rhythm of creation, which in Hindu philosophy is called "the Breath of Brahma"; the outflowing breath causing the universe and the ingoing breath dissolving it into unity once more. It is interesting to note how many words, embodying the idea "spirit" are at the same time connected with the idea of "breath". There is the Sanskrit word *Atma*, the Hebrew *Ruach*, the Greek *Pneuma*, the Latin *Spiritus* and our own English word *spirit*, all of which either mean breath or are closely connected with that idea.

This divine Breath then is the rhythm of creation which is the very nature of the Divine and which therefore can be found in all things, in all cycles of manifestation from the greatest to the smallest. The cyclic process of creation is the fundamental law of this universe, and all our cycles of time, the *yugas* of the Hindu philosophers, all periods of evolution are manifestations of that one eternal cycle of creation, in which and through which the universe exists.

Thus the awakening of a universe from the unity of *pralaya*, its existence in diversity during a *manvantara* of outer manifestation, and its return through that manifestation to the unity of divine Being is the greatest of these cycles of creation, but, as in this greatest period of time, so also in the small period of one single day the eternal rhythm of creation can be found.

At dawn, the world awakens from the unity of the night to the manifoldness of outer activity, and in the sunrise there is a sense of exultant life being reborn after the night of rest. At noon the struggle of outer activity, the clash of the many striving and toiling creatures, is at its highest. But in the evening, the work of the day being over, the world returns to rest, and there is a peace in sunset which, like a balm, heals the wounds of strife. In that moment, when the sun disappears behind the horizon, it is as if the entire world were united in the worship of God; all creatures seem to be drawn together in the harmony of the spirit, and once more a world, weary with toil and suffering, returns to the divine rest from which it awakened at dawn; the Breath of creation returns.

As it is in the cycle of one single day, so once again we find the rhythm of creation in the cycle of the year. In spring, the outer world awakens from the unity and rest of winter, and with all the joy and vitality of youth nature is reborn; in midsummer, the diversity of outer manifestation is at its fullest, the world, nature, is glorified; and in autumn, the return to unity begins—there is a gentle melancholy in autumn, a peace not found in spring, in which all things seem to return to the one Life of God from which they came. Then, in winter, all is at rest once more, and the unity of the spirit asserts itself while life seems to be withdrawn from outer nature. The Breath of creation has returned; for the moment all things are one with God, and in the deepest midnight of winter, the midnight of Christmas, when all nature is silent, Christ, the divine Child, is born anew. It is a deeply significant fact that the birth of the Christ should have been placed at this moment of the year, when the Spirit within is manifest and nature without appears to be dead.

THE CYCLE OF HUMAN LIFE

In the life of man the same eternal rhythm of creation is manifest. The child is as yet one with the divine life; there is a harmony and grace in childhood which is lost as the child grows up. With the awakening of individuality the soul estranges itself from the divine unity and becomes the separate creature, fighting for self in the fullness of individual development. But in old age we sometimes see that wonderful return to unity, when a gentle and wise peace seems to descend on the soul which has completed its cycle of existence.

The life of a human being is but a day in the greater life of the eternal spirit which is the true self of man. In this greater life, this pilgrimage of the soul, we again see the rhythm of creation manifest; in the course of many lives on earth the soul travels from unity in God through ages of suffering in matter—a crucifixion in the world of outer existence—back to God from whom it came, but now in full self-consciousness, bearing with it the harvest of its ages of suffering.

THE SONG OF CREATION

Thus, everywhere, we find the same eternal Breath of creation; the outbreathing into manifestation and diversity, the return towards the unity of divine Life. It is the song of creation, the song which God sings, of which all songs in this universe are part. Every creature, every object, every atom of matter, all that is and all that happens, is a note in that great symphony of creation. It is the song of God the Holy Ghost, the song which sings in our souls as well as in the smallest atom. Once we have heard that song of creation, the world can never again be ugly or evil; what we call evil or ugliness is but our inability to hear the apparent discord dissolved in the greater harmony of the creative rhythm. It is only when within our consciousness we have heard the song of God the Holy Ghost, that we can hear it everywhere around us, and that the entire universe, with its millions of creatures, its ceaseless activity, its apparent discord and disharmony, all its suffering and misery, is dissolved in the one throbbing harmony of the song of creation. Nothing then remains but that one majestic rhythm, in which we all exist as notes in a great symphony. It is the rhythm of the world, the rhythm of our human soul, the rhythm of life.

THE THREE STAGES OF CREATION

In the great cycle of creation we can distinguish three main periods: the first where creation is still in the divine life, and where the unity of that life still prevails in its manifestations; second, a stage in which the Breath of creation has gone forth to its uttermost limits, and where the unity of life is lost in the diversity of outer existence; and third, the stage in which the divine life after its crucifixion in matter returns to itself, but now in the full self-consciousness gained through long ages of evolution through separate forms.

We call the first stage that of nature, and it is a stage in which the divine life identifies itself with the whole of created forms in all their countless diversities, and not with any one in particular. Therefore there is no individuality in nature; the harmony of the one divine will can sweep through the world of forms and be manifest as natural law, without meeting the obstruction of any separate wills. There is a unity, a harmony in nature, in which all its separate forms and creatures seem to blend into one great coordinated whole, in which all the struggle and strife of Nature, "red in tooth and claw" as she may be, seems to dissolve. The reason why creation in nature is so beautiful and harmonious is that God's creative activity can manifest through it unhindered; the separate creature in nature does not pretend to be a creator, and therefore there is no danger of the divine beauty being marred by individual discords. Even the countless beings belonging to the so-called Angelic kingdom, elementals, nature-spirits and Angels or Devas, are never individually creative, but are always part of the one creative activity of God.

UNITY IN NATURE

We must be careful not to overestimate the apparent harmonious cooperation of creatures in nature. When studying the life of bees or ants, we cannot help admiring the perfect coordination of their communal existence, and sometimes we are apt to compare it to the chaos of our human social life, much to the disadvantage of the latter. Such a comparison, however, is not just; the unity of nature is not the result of the willing and conscious cooperation of separate individuals, but is possible only because there is as yet no individuality to mar the unity of the whole. Thus nature is a stage of unconscious unity in which the divine creative activity can work its purpose without obstruction.

THE SECOND STAGE—CULTURE

All these things change with individualization. When the individual emerges from the group soul, the separate will begins to assert itself, and from that moment thè divine unity, the wonder of nature, is lost, the harmony and beauty of natural life disappear, and instead come disharmony, chaos and confusion. Whereas, in nature, the only creative activity is that of God, and the separate creature does not attempt to work its own scheme of creation, the situation is different when man appears on the stage, and the harmony of nature gives way to the disharmony of culture. For as "nature" (from the Latin *natura*) means the stage in which the birth of the separate creature within the species determines its significance, so the stage of culture (Latin *colo,* I cultivate) is that in which the separate individual begins to cultivate, to re-create the world surrounding him. Man, however, is not as good a creator as God, and where man tries to improve on

God's handiwork in nature the result is not satisfactory. There is an artificiality in all man's creations, a following of his own individual schemes and inclinations, regardless of the plan and purposes of the greater whole, which causes the often appalling ugliness and disharmony of our human existence. We need but study the streets of our modern cities to find evidence of this individualistic lust of separate creations; each house is the plan of some individual trying to follow his own ideas of utility and beauty, without the slightest consideration of the way in which his neighbors have tried to realize theirs. The result, however meritorious the individual efforts may be, is always disastrous. In nature the traces of man's culture are ever destructive; God makes and man mars the beauty of natural life.

All this is a necessary stage. The individual must develop the powers and faculties of his own apparently separate self, before he can return in full self-consciousness to the divine life which is his by right, and claim the divinity of which he was but oblivious for a while. Thus the moment comes when man realizes the futility of his illusion of separateness, of his desire to possess outer things, power, or riches, for a separate self which is unreal; the moment comes when the fruits of desire turn to ashes in the mouth, and when in utter weariness, in utter despair, man abandons the pursuit of the outer world and turns inward. It is then, in the silence of the soul, that the voice of the spirit can speak to man, and that he within his own consciousness can hear the great song of creation. From that moment man grows toward unity; he now offers the powers he has developed in his long pilgrimage on the altar of service to his fellow men; more and more he tries to harmonize his separate will with the one will of God, until finally he gains utter freedom, the only possible freedom, by merging his will in that divine will, or rather by discovering that his separate will was but an illusion and that there is nothing but the one divine will in the entire universe. Through ages of sustained effort, man thus regains the unity of the divine life, but it is only when man becomes an Adept that he finally and entirely transcends the stage of culture in order to enter that of superhuman or divine creative activity.

The Third Stage—Deification

Once more God's creative activity can realize itself in this third stage without meeting any obstacle or obstruction, once again there is perfect harmony and unity, but now it is no longer the unconscious coordination of nature, in which there is as yet no individuality to mar the unity; it is the splendid and fully conscious cooperation of superhuman beings, who, having ended their human evolution and become conscious of their own divinity, fully realize their unity with God. They are now consciously part of the divine life and activity; their nature, like God's nature, is to be creative, and it is through these countless thousands of superhuman beings that God's eternal creative activity takes place.

In this divine creative Hierarchy there is but one will, one purpose. No rules, no laws, no outer government are necessary to ensure obedience and cooperation; all are as conscious cells in the one great living being we call God, working in perfect unison, living but to serve His purpose, which in the deepest and truest sense is their own divine will.

Thus the great rhythm of life, the Breath of creation, has returned to God the Holy Ghost through whom it went forth; the cycle of manifestation has been completed. It is in this great cyclic law of evolution, with its ever-recurring three stages in the greater as well as in the smaller cycles, that we can see the Holy Spirit manifest as the eternal Breath, by which and in which exists all that lives.

IV THE DIVINE RITUAL

In the theological conception of creation, we not only meet with a conception of God's creative activity as an action having taken place only once upon a time, but we also find a conception of God as a single being realizing His purpose alone and through Himself. Now that conception is true if only we can keep in mind that God is One and Many at the same time, that just as the Trinity does not mar the unity of the Godhead, so also the fact that each of the three Persons of the divine Trinity is a Hierarchy of superhuman beings, does not take away anything from the unity of each. God is the Creator, but His creative activity is realized through many millions of beings, who form the great creative Hierarchies, carrying God's power to the smallest creatures and forms in His manifested universe, each and every one of which is under the care of some being, who either forms part of the great creative Hierarchy, or else works under the supervision and orders of a member of that Hierarchy. Through the creative Hierarchy the rhythm of creation is realized; through it that daily Eucharist takes place in which God Himself "as the eternal High Priest forever offers Himself as the eternal Sacrifice," that daily Eucharist in which eternally all nature is consecrated by the divine life flowing into it, and in which all separate beings continually regain that unity within, the true Communion, which is the end of the great rhythm of creation.

THE GRAND LODGE ABOVE

The creative Hierarchy is that body of which we read in the rituals of that great repository of occult teaching, Free-masonry, the eternal Grand Lodge which has the Father, Son, and Holy Ghost as its principal Officers, the universe for its Temple, the heavens for its celestial Canopy and all created things for its Tessellated Pavement. It is there that the grand and eternal ritual of creation takes place, ever-lasting, incessant, for without it the universe could not exist. It is in that grand ritual above that those who have become superhuman, who have reentered the divine life in full self-consciousness, take part; it is when man has become divine that he becomes creative, becomes part of that great ritual of creation. All rituals here below, the rituals of the great world religions as well as those of Freemasonry and similar bodies, are based on that one grand ritual above, and it is through our rituals here below that we can even now partake in God's work of creation, which will be ours some day when we have become supermen. Thus in ritual the magnificent and un-paralleled opportunity is given to man to be more than man, to be divine in creative activity.

THE MEANING OF RITUAL

To most people ritual seems a waste of time, they recog-nize that certain ethical truths may be taught in the guise of symbols, they recognize that through symbols and ritualistic actions certain philosophical teachings may be understood, but they wonder why such ethics and philosophy are not taught in a plain and straightforward way, instead of being carefully hidden in the various forms and actions of ceremo-nial and ritual? This seems a logical objection to ritual, but in reality it is but a misunderstanding of its true meaning. Apart from the fact that in ritual man undergoes the psychological effect of the actions performed, and so experiences as a reality in his consciousness that which in ordinary ethical and philosophical teachings can only be told in words, apart from the fact that in ritual man symbolically partakes in the reality of things which he cannot yet bear in their undisguised full-ness, ritual has one great and supreme meaning, which is that in and through it man, even while he is but man, can share in the work of God the Holy Ghost, the work of world creation. It may seem almost incredible that such a tremendous work should be possible for human beings; but it is not for nothing that Freemasonry has ever called itself the Royal Art, and that the sacrifice of the Holy Eucharist, the supreme ritual of the Christian Church, has ever been surrounded by an un-paralleled reverence and awe.

All great rituals are based on the one primordial ritual, and are so linked up to that divine ritual of creation, that every action in the ritual here below corresponds to some very much greater reality in that eternal ritual above. Thus from our human ceremonial, a constant stream goes up to join that mighty flood of creative fire which is the manifestation of God the Holy Ghost, while on the other hand the ritual performed on earth, being as it were attuned to the grand ritual above, can transmit something of the divine creative forces to the world surrounding the place where it is per-formed.

THE HOLY EUCHARIST

When in the ritual of the Liberal Catholic Church, after the Consecration of the Elements, the priest prays that our obla-tion may be carried to the Altar of God on high, "there to be offered by Him, who as the eternal High Priest forever offers Himself as the eternal Sacrifice," the result is that through the channel made by the act of consecration between the elements of bread and wine on earth and the very being of God Himself, those who partake in the ritual, and who offer themselves and the divine work or theurgy in which they are engaged in utter dedication to God, for a moment partake in the divine ritual, and contribute their small human stream of force to the divine forces of creation.

In the ritual of the Holy Eucharist the entire rhythm of creation is followed, the descent of the divine life into matter takes place once more in the consecration of the elements, and the return to unity of the divine life is effected in that communion which is the consummation of the creative rhythm as well as of the Eucharistic Service.

THE MASONIC RITUAL

In a similar manner the Masonic ritual is based on the grand ritual above, and in it we touch the activity of God the Holy Ghost even more closely than in the Christian ritual, for the latter is centered round the Second Person of the Trinity, God the Son, the Christ, who is the heart and life of the Christian religion. Yet insofar as the Christian ritual allows us to partake of the divine work of creation and, in that magnificent moment after the Consecration, enables us to pour our own small force into the very heart of the creative activity, we share in the work of God the Holy Spirit as well as in that of the Second Person of the Trinity.

In Freemasonry with its building symbolism, all is centered round the work of God the Creator, God the Holy Ghost. In the opening and closing of the masonic lodge the divine Ritual of creation is followed step by step, and each action has a cosmic significance far beyond our grandest conceptions of the importance of the ritual in which we are engaged.

Truly, there is no work in ordinary life, however great it may seem on the physical plane, however magnificent its immediate physical result may appear to be, which can compare to the greatness of this ritual work. In it alone man is divine in his activity, in it alone he can share in God's ritual of creation and do a work for which, being merely man, he is not in reality yet fully prepared, the work which will be his only when he consciously enters the great creative Hierarchy.

In ritual we thus share in the work of God the Holy Ghost; we assist in that daily reconsecration of the universe by which all life is maintained; we are for a moment more than man—divine. It may seem hard to understand that any group of mere human beings should be able to share in and add anything to the divine work, but we must remember always that God is One and also Many, that God is not separate from

His universe or from humanity, but that we are in very truth God, that every atom of our bodies, every fiber of our souls is divine, utterly and entirely divine. Thus while we share in the work of God, we do but anticipate that work which one day must be entirely ours when we have claimed the divinity of which now we are oblivious, when we have reentered the divine life from which we came.

V THE DYNAMIC UNIVERSE

The universe of God the Holy Spirit is a dynamic universe, a universe of which *dynamis* or power is the keynote. There is a great difference between the static view of the universe and the dynamic view—the one embodying construction, the other movement. We can best understand that difference when considering, for instance, the human form from the static and then from the dynamic point of view. From the static point of view we see the construction of the human organism; we can analyze how the body is built up, which organs are to be found in it; we can draw the outline and indicate the texture of each organ and part of the body, and thus gain a conception of the entire creature as it is at one particular instant of time. We crystallize the living human form as it were into a frozen immobility, and give a description of how it is in that state.

If, on the other hand, we look at the human body from the dynamic point of view we see it as moving, growing, and evolving; we do not merely describe the construction of any part, but first and foremost the *function* of it. Thus, for instance, when considering the heart we should first see the function of the heart, its meaning and action in the organism; and its shape, construction and texture would have meaning to us only as expressing the function for which it is to serve.

We can readily see that the dynamic view is a very much more living one than the static view. The latter ignores the life side by which the form side is determined; it begins by introducing the fiction of immobility in that which it considers, and consequently misses the function which after all is the purpose any object or creature serves in life.

For many centuries most subjects of study have been looked at from the static point of view, and it is only recently that the dynamic point of view is becoming more prominent. This is another sign of the advent of the age of the Holy Ghost, for the dynamic standpoint is the standpoint of the Holy Spirit, the standpoint of creative activity, of change, of growth and evolution, the standpoint of time.

The Dynamic View in the Theory of Evolution

One of the symptoms of this dynamic view of the universe has been the theory of evolution, which has become so thoroughly a part of our general outlook during the last century. We cannot now imagine what the universe would look like without the concept of evolution. Nature around us, the world of forms, would be merely a chaotic collection of many millions of forms, not in any way causally connected, but "just there," existing in their particular way since their creation by God, or, if we do not accept the orthodox view, thrown together by the accident of material circumstances. With the introduction of the dynamic or evolutionary standpoint, these millions of different forms suddenly become coordinated; we recognize their evolution from simple to complex forms; we can watch how from the main line of evolution different branches have gone forth, and how each of these different species and creatures appear, all causally connected with the main current of evolution. From this standpoint we never see any form as "just there," by itself, but always as the result of past evolution, and the cause of future forms. The moment, for instance, we think of the human form, we instantly realize the forms that have gone before and of which it is the consummation, and furthermore we can see it as a step towards even higher forms. But we cannot possibly consider it by itself, disconnected from all that has gone before and all that is to follow.

THE EVOLUTION OF LIFE

Whereas, however, the conception of evolution of form has become almost common property, the idea of the evolution of *life* is still far from being universally recognized; and yet it is as important, if not more important, a reality than the former. Here, again, instead of seeing the millions of different manifestations of life around us and in us, and taking them for granted as just being there, whether by a special creation of God or by the chance of circumstances, we see every manifestation of life as part of the great process of the evolution of life, and evolution leading from less complete manifestations of the Divine to fuller ones.

It has been one of the main contributions of Theosophy that it has coordinated the entire universe in one great conception of the evolution of life. Just as the evolution of form shows our own physical form to be the outcome of a long process of physical evolution, so in the evolution of life, the life within us is seen as the outcome of an age long evolution from the very simplest manifestations to ever higher and higher stages, until in the great rhythm of creation the separate life has regained the unity of the Divine from which it came.

The dynamic view of the universe applied to the human soul, to our own life, the consciousness within us, produces as its result the doctrine of Reincarnation, of the many lives on earth through which we have reached our present stage of evolution, the doctrine of Karma by which our different lives are causally connected, and the doctrine of the Perfection or Deification of man, in which that life reaches its perfection.

It is not only in the realm of biology or religion that this dynamic conception of the universe has become so much more prominent of late; in all departments of life—in art and science as well as in economics or politics—the tendency of the age is never to look at any form or institution as just there, existing by itself, but always as part of some evolutionary process, the result of some creative energy. Thus everywhere the universe of the Holy Ghost is becoming more and more a recognized reality; we are beginning to see all things and all creatures as part of the great rhythm of creation which is His manifestation.

PRESENT, PAST AND FUTURE NONEXISTING?

Gradually, as we gain the dynamic standpoint, the entire history, or cycle of evolution, of any particular thing, being, or movement becomes much more real to us than any separate moment of its history. In reality there is no such thing as a being at any particular moment of time. When, for instance, we ask ourselves who we are, and think that we have solved this question by saying we are the being who is here now at this moment in this room, we have to realize that even while we say the word "now" the being, which existed here in that fraction of a second, has already become part of the past which no longer exists. Similarly the being which is to exist in another fraction of a second is not yet there, that is to say it is nonexistent too at the present time. And the present moment itself is fugitive, intangible; the moment we think of it, it is already gone and the next moment has come. In fact what we call the present has no definite dimension in time; it is a mathematical line which distinguishes what we call past and future, but it has no real existence of its own. Thus we are in this absurd position that the present "we" are nonexistent because the present has no dimension; the past "we" are no longer existent, and the future "we" do not yet exist—which means, if we add the sum total of these different nothingnesses, that we do not exist at all, which of course is absurd.

SOLUTION OF THE PROBLEM

The moment we gain the dynamic standpoint, that is to say when we look at any being or thing from the standpoint of the Holy Spirit, our difficulty vanishes. From that point of view the real being is that which covers its whole history from the very beginning to the very end. Thus any one of us is in reality that which we have been from the earliest moment of our existence to the very end of our appearance as a separate creature, and what we call "ourselves" at the present moment is only the ever-shifting cross section of that real creature. To say that the past is past and the future is not yet, but that the present exists, is entirely wrong. It is rather the other way round; the past and future together are the real being, and what we call the present is but a shifting sectional view of that being as it exists in reality. Thus in the dynamic universe of the Holy Ghost every creature, every object, every event, every social movement, every period of history, exists in its entirety, not as the sum total of all the different cross sections—appearing one after another as the successive stages of growth of that being or movement—but as the real being, in whom all that we call past and all that we call future is always present.

It is not possible to grasp with the intellect that which belongs to the world of the divine Mind which is above the intellect, and in a following chapter I hope to explain the difference between the perception of the Real by the higher mind and the interpretation of that perception by the instrument which we call the intellect. Thus, intellectually, we cannot conceive of the entirety of a being as it exists in the universe seen from the dynamic standpoint, and still less can we understand how all that we call movement, change, growth, or evolution is an abiding reality at that level. But we can experience it when we come in touch with the Holy Spirit, for the dynamic standpoint is his standpoint; time, evolution, history, cycles of manifestation are all part of the rhythm of creation which is his very being.

LOOKING UP THE FUTURE

We have all heard of the possibility of looking up the records of the past, the so-called *akashic* records, and in them experiencing events which we would call past as still happening, as still present. When once we understand the dynamic standpoint of the universe, there is no longer any absurdity about this. But neither is there any improbability in looking up the records of the future; there is no more unreality about the future than there is about the past, future and past being but clumsy terms which we give to the different parts of a real being of which we know only the cross-section we call the present. It is not true that the past is gone and that the future is not yet; past and future are the one and only real present, and what we call present is the only thing which does not exist. Many people try to look up their past lives and are interested in what they have and have not been, but how much more glorious would their experience be if they attempted to look up the future! We are all supposed to be evolving and our future is, as it has been expressed so beautifully, "the future of a thing whose growth and splendor have no limit." We are all to be Adepts in the future, and that future greatness of every one of us is a reality which exists now, as much as the earlier stages of our evolution exist now, and instead of inspiring ourselves with the imperfections from which we have evolved, we might do better to try to contact the perfection which one day must be ours.

INSPIRATION FROM THE FUTURE

Now we might say that, though we find some people who are able to look up the past, we find few if any who are able to look up the future, which would seem to prove that the future is not available in the same way as the past is. But then we must remember that most people do not believe in the reality of the future, but cannot help believing in the reality of the past, the results of which they continually meet. We think of the past as having happened, and it agrees with our common sense that one can look up such a past. The imagination of most people can be stretched so far as to recognize the possibility of reviving the impressions once made by events in the past, but they would draw the line at the suggestion that the records of the future are present in exactly the same way as the records of the past. Yet there is no greater absurdity in looking up the future than there is in looking up the past, and on the whole we should benefit very much more by it. Our real being covers our entire evolution; and, if we can come in touch with that stage of it in which we are the perfect Man, that contact cannot fail to be a continual help and inspiration to us at the present moment. In fact, as I hope to show in a later chapter, the nature of what we call inspiration is this coming in touch with the real being in the dynamic universe and contacting the creative energy which causes it to accomplish what we call its entire cycle of evolution. If thus we come in touch with the future of any movement, or with that of any nation, or with any period in art, or scheme of social or political reform, we are thrilled with the dynamic energy which is evolving such a movement or such a nation towards what we call its future, and we are filled with what we call inspiration or enthusiasm to work toward that future.

THE UNIVERSE OF GOD THE HOLY SPIRIT

It is easy to realize how important for our daily life is this dynamic view of the universe, this universe of the Holy Spirit. It enables us to touch everything in its energy aspect, to contact, as it were, the creative power which is to carry it toward its perfection. In this contact we ourselves become filled with the creative energy of the Holy Spirit, we are touched by the fire of creation and are able to achieve things of which as mere individuals we should be entirely incapable. It is this contact with the dynamic universe which makes the prophet and seer, the enthusiast and reformer, the life bringer in all the different departments of our existence. It is not for nothing that one of the gifts of the Holy Ghost is the gift of prophecy. In the creative rhythm, which is the manifestation of the Holy Spirit, past and future are an ever-present reality.

The knowledge of the great cycle of creation, and its manifestation in the countless smaller cycles in the history of nature as well as in that of races, nations, and human beings, belongs to this great department of the Holy Spirit. One of its manifestations in human knowledge is the science of astrology, not in its commoner form of "fortune-telling," but in its deep and esoteric meaning of the knowledge of cosmic cycles of evolution and the ways in which the lives of nations and individuals are interwoven with them. It is not for nothing that this true science is not popularly known, and that the *Yuga* doctrine of the Hindus is found in statements so veiled that one can hardly unravel their true meaning. For the knowledge of all the cycles of evolution bestows the gift of prophesying the future; knowing the nature of an entire cycle of evolution, and knowing that part of it which, in what we call time, has already been traversed, we can with absolute certainty predict its future; and such prediction is not without its dangers.

IMPORTANCE OF THE DYNAMIC VIEW

It is hardly possible to overestimate the possibilities of the dynamic view of the universe. Every object, every creature, every event, every period of time, is here seen as part of the eternal rhythm of creation, in which all the millions of larger and smaller cycles of evolution are as the different chords which make up the great symphony of the universe. It is a symphony in which every note is vibrant with creative energy, of which every chord has power to create or to destroy. Every one of us is a note or a chord in that symphony, and when we come in touch with our chord we can gain the creative inspiration of our entire cycle of evolution. Thus we not only come to a deeper knowledge of what we in reality are, but we can even now be inspired by that which we are to become one day in what we call the future.

Our entire world becomes transformed and energized when we begin to see it as part of the dynamic universe of creation; we begin to live in a world of life, ever changing, moving and growing, a world, creative in every atom: the world of the Holy Spirit.

VI DIVINE ALCHEMY

There is only one creative energy in the universe, and that is the power of God the Holy Ghost. All that we call force or energy, whether within us or in nature around us, is but a mode of that one eternal, creative power of God. Thus it is the creative activity of the Third Logos, of God the Holy Ghost, which sets up the vortex of stellar matter which is the beginning of a universe; it is this creative power which sets up that fundamental vortex of energy which we call the ultimate atom; it is in the laboratory of God the Holy Ghost, the *Demiurge*—the *Ptah* of the Egyptians and *Vulcan* of Roman mythology—that the divine chemistry takes place, which is the basis of our material universe. Let us never forget that if but for a moment that creative activity were withdrawn, if but for an instant the creative energy of the Holy Ghost ceased to flow into the universe, in the ultimate atom as well as in the stellar nebula, there would be no physical world left. It is the incessant re-creation of the world by the Creator which maintains it as it is, and we verily owe our physical existence to God the Holy Ghost.

ALCHEMY AND THE MAGNUM OPUS

It is curious to note how modern science, though it has advanced far beyond the ancient conceptions of matter and force, has yet lost some of the deeper knowledge which man in olden times possessed with regard to the activity of the Holy Ghost as the divine alchemist. There is a science of the

work of the Holy Ghost with what we call the chemical
elements and their interrelation, which from Egypt, through
Ancient Greece and Arabia, reached Europe in the early
Middle Ages under the name of *Alchemy*, and, though its
students had but very primitive notions of what today we call
chemistry, they yet knew some fundamental facts about the
inner nature of matter and the elements. It was this knowledge which enabled the alchemists to perform what was
called the *magnum opus,* the great work, in which, as they
expressed it in their quaint language, "the quintessence was
drawn from the lower metals," and by its aid the silver was
transmuted into gold. There is no doubt that there were many
thousands of pseudoalchemists in the Middle Ages, who had
only their strange jargon in common with the true alchemists,
and entirely lacked their deeper knowledge; and the abundance of worthless literature with which they flooded the
world has seriously damaged the appreciation of the true
Hermetic mystery of real alchemy. But to the earnest student
it becomes soon possible to distinguish at a glance between
the real and the unreal in this literary material, and by collect-
ing the works of true alchemists and Rosicrucians and by
studying them with the proper key for their interpretation, we
come to realize something of the vast knowledge they had of
the working of the one creative energy in matter.

THE SECRET SYMBOLS OF THE ROSICRUCIANS

There is a wonderfully interesting book which was published by the Brothers of the Golden and Rosy Cross—a later
development of the original Rosicrucian Brotherhood
—which is called *Geheime Figuren der Rosenkreuzer aus
dem 16ten und 17ten Jahrhundert,* published in 1785 in Al-
tona, in which a great deal of this inner knowledge of real
alchemy is to be found by those who can interpret the profound symbols of which the book is composed. I do not know
of any book which can bring one nearer to that marvelous
knowledge of the old Rosicrucians with regard to the workings of the divine creative energy in nature and in man, and
anyone who makes a really earnest study of this marvelous

work will find himself well repaid. The book was partially republished in an English translation by Dr. Franz Hartmann in 1888 in Boston. A complete edition of the original German work was published in 1919 by Hermann Barsdorf in Berlin, and thus this wonderful ancient wisdom is once more open to modern students.

THE MAGNUM OPUS IN MAN

The marvelous part of the ancient presentation of these truths is that they held good, not only for the transmutations in nature which a knowledge of the creative power can effect, but also for the transmutation, the *magnum opus,* to be accomplished in man himself. In several alchemical works we find it expressly mentioned that the highest aim of alchemy was the transmutation of the creative power in man, and that the application of that knowledge to physical nature was but a minor department of their great science. Thus, when we read in these ancient works that man must draw the quintessence from the lower metals and with its aid transmute the silver into gold, or again when we read how by the aid of the power hidden in the center of the earth the moon must become the sun, these statements hold good as well for transmutations of matter to be accomplished in the laboratory of the alchemist, as for that inner transmutation which is to take place in the laboratory of man's own nature, in the crucible of the soul. In this latter interpretation the baser metals are man's earthly desires and passions, and to draw the quintessence from these lower matters means to liberate the creative energy in our own nature from its entanglements in the world of the senses. With the aid of that liberated creative energy the silver of the soul can be transmuted into the gold of the spirit, or, using the other terminology, by the aid of the power drawn from the *center of the earth,* the moon, that is to say the soul, can become the sun, which is the spirit.

KUNDALINI, THE MANIFESTATION OF THE HOLY GHOST

The ancient alchemist knew of that creative power in man

which in Hindu philosophy is called the *kundalini,* or serpent-fire. In a very interesting little book by Johann Gichtel, a disciple of the famous Jacob Boehme, called *Theosophia Practica,* we find an interesting picture which shows the body of a man with the serpent-fire coiled up at the base of the spine in the shape of a dragon, and the different centers or *chakras* in the body indicated as the parts through which that serpent-fire has to be guided. This turning inward and upward of the central creative energy in man, which in its lower manifestation is turned outward as sex desire, is that same *magnum opus* or divine transmutation which was the goal of the true alchemist.

There is only one creative power in the universe, and that is the power of God the Holy Ghost. In man, one of its manifestations is sexual desire; man in the earlier stages of his evolution turns the great creative energy within himself to the world of matter surrounding him, and seeks union in the world of diversities. It is only through suffering that he finally discovers that there is no union but the ever-abiding unity of the spirit. However, even in those earlier stages of evolution it is in the mystery of sex that man can create, that in him the creative energy of God the Holy Ghost is manifest. But as man evolves, he learns how to transmute that desire of sex to ever higher and higher levels, so that successively he becomes creative in the world of the emotions, in the world of the mind, and finally in the world of the spirit. It is the same creative energy which inspires the great work of art, or which enables the philosopher or scientist to give his contribution to humanity, and by which the social reformer and humanist is able to better the lot of his fellow men, that, in its lower manifestation, was the creative energy of sex, and it is by the transmutation and not by the repression of our earthly desires and passions that we can become creative at higher levels. There is a deep truth in the old alchemical formula which teaches man not to destroy the lower metals but to draw their quintessence, and with the aid of that quintessence, that is to say, with the aid of the divine creative energy hidden in his passions and desires, to transmute his humanity into divinity.

THE SACREDNESS OF SEX

For many centuries the entire subject of sex has been looked upon as unworthy of consideration; the manifestations of creative energy in the realm of sex have been ignored and where possible repressed, and the entire subject has been surrounded by a false shame which made it impossible to shed any light on its true importance in the life of man. It is not in this way that we can accomplish the *magnum opus* or divine transmutation; it is not by looking upon sex as a necessarily base and unworthy subject that we can release the divine creative energy which in it is turned outward and downward, instead of inward and upward; and it is only when we begin to teach our children that the creative power of sex is a divine force, the one divine power given to all men alike, that we can hope to lift the entire subject of sex out of the mire of sensuality and lust in which it is now obscured, and to show it in its true and splendid meaning.

The misconceptions and abuses of the creative powers in man are that true sin against the Holy Ghost which is so little understood. In the humanity of the future, the creative power of sex and the mystery of the procreation of the human race by the union of man and woman will be taught as a sacred Mystery; and that union itself will no longer be a gratification of the lust of the moment, but will become a prayer to the human soul for whom in this manner an earthly tabernacle is to be prepared. It is only then that a nobler and truer human race can be produced; and, once more, the solution of the mystery lies in the old alchemical formula of transmutation, and not in the current, though never successful, practice of repression.

THE TRANSMUTATION OF SEX DESIRE

Thus, even in its earthly manifestation as the creative power of sex, the presence of that great power of God the Holy Ghost in man can be a very holy and pure subject. But the possibilities are even greater when evolving man begins to transmute that power into higher forms of creative activity.

Far from being dismayed by the desires and passions which we meet with in ourselves, we must face them frankly, and recognize that in them and in the creative energy manifest in them lies our opportunity of being creative at higher levels. It is not the man without passion or desire who can ever become greatly creative, nor the man who allows his desires and passions to control him, but he who having a strong passion nature is able to draw the quintessence from the baser metals, that is to say, liberate the creative energy from its lower entanglements and lead it *upward* so that it becomes the creative power of the spirit. A foreceful nature can be greatly bad, but at least it offers the possibility of becoming greatly good, but a nature without force is too weak and insignificant to be either bad or good. It is not for nothing that the lukewarm souls are condemned in Revelation, and were not only barred from Dante's *Paradiso* and *Purgatorio,* but were not even admitted in the *Inferno.*

The Holy Ghost as Purifier

We can now understand how the Holy Ghost is also the great Purifier. It is that divine Fire of creation within us which, though in the earlier stages it manifests only at lower levels, gradually burns all earthly dross out of our nature, and enables us to effect the great transmutation to ever higher levels, until finally nothing but the pure gold of the spirit remains. One of the gifts of the Holy Spirit in the Christian Church has ever been that of driving out all uncleanliness, of exorcising and purifying and helping man in that great work of transmuting his earthly desires so that they become the desire of the Divine.

Psychoanalysis a Partial View

It is interesting to see how modern psychology has approached the same subject and come to the same conclusion from a materialistic standpoint. Psychoanalysis, too, recognizes that there is only one creative energy in man of which all his desires, passions and aspirations are but different modes. It calls this central urge the *libido* and recognizes the desire of sex as its central manifestation.* It, too, recognizes the necessity of a transmutation of this *libido* to higher levels, but it rarely succeeds in accomplishing this sublimation or introversion in a satisfactory manner. The reason is that psychoanalysis, or at least the older school of psycho-analysts, looks upon sex desire, the *libido,* as the fundamental and original creative energy, and upon all higher creative effort as merely a higher mode of manifestation of that *libido* or sex desire. We, on the other hand, look upon sex desire and the creative power of sex as a merely physical manifesta-tion, a turning outwards, of the divine creative Energy in man, which is the power of God the Holy Ghost. Thus we look upon the transmutation of this energy as *the return of the divine creative power to the level where it belongs,* whereas the psychoanalyst of the Freudian type looks upon all higher manifestation of the creative power as sublimated modes of a power which has its original and true level on the physical plane, in what we call sex desire. This is a very fundamental difference; we look upon the material power as a temporary aberration of a divine and spiritual energy, whereas these psychoanalysts look upon all higher creative energy as a temporary manifestation of a power which has its true home in the physical world as the creative power of sex. We might say that this form of psychoanalysis is the materialistic or upside-down presentation of the true doctrine of the creative energy of God the Holy Ghost and the divine Alchemy by which that power is to be released.

ALCHEMIST AND PSYCHOANALYST

The medieval alchemist and the modern psychoanalyst thus often speak the same language, but mean entirely differ-ent things. A psychoanalyst like Silberer, for instance, in his book *Problem der Mystik und ihrer Symbolik,* when discuss-

---

* Developments in psychology since this book was written have given the term *libido* a much broader meaning than indicated here. Today it refers to the total psychic energy of man, at whatever level it may be operating. Ed.

ing the alchemical and Rosicrucian teachings with regard to the process of transmutation, interprets whatever the alchemists say on the subject from his own materialistic standpoint, using the same terminology, but always looking at the problem from below instead of from above.

It is clear that the *magnum opus* can never be accomplished until and unless we recognize that our lower, physical desires and passions are temporary manifestations of the divine creative energy; only then is there any chance of our releasing that imprisoned creative power and making it available at the levels to which it belongs. Psychoanalysts—at least those who look upon the material manifestation of creative energy as the fundamental reality and upon all higher creative effort as a sublimation of these material realities —can never fully accomplish the true transmutation. The final transmutation, the *magnum opus* of the Rosicrucians and alchemists, requires above all not only a belief but a certainty of spiritual and divine things as primary and of material things as secondary, the lower being a manifestation of the higher and not the higher of the lower. We must first be established in the reality of spiritual things, if we would lift the imprisoned forces of our lower nature to those higher levels; and unless the psychoanalyst himself stands on those levels, he cannot possibly assist his patients to accomplish the work of sublimation; and he may even become a deadly danger to his victims, when, after having brought their hidden complexes into the open and released the *libido,* he fails to make them transmute that *libido* into divine creative activity. The Road of psychoanalysis is strewn with the wrecks of the unhappy subjects in whom the *libido* has been awakened, but not transmuted.

PSYCHOANALYSIS AND THE OCCULT PATH

The only one who can accomplish safely the work, which the psychoanalyst so often attempts in a blundering way, is the Master of the Wisdom in the training of his pupil. He alone knows how much of the hidden complexes or *skandhas* he can safely bring to the surface in the consciousness of his pupil; he alone is able to watch the progress of that pupil and

see exactly how much he can bear in the work of transmutation; and finally he alone can safely release the creative
energy, the serpent-fire or *kundalini,* and lead it inward and
upward through the different centers of the body so that man
may become spiritually creative. Psychoanalysis, insofar as
it attempts the great transmutation, is often but the materialistic semblance of the occult path. It is immensely valuable in dealing with cases of abnormal psychology, but it is
insufficient to accomplish that final consummation of human
evolution which alchemists call the *magnum opus,* the great
work.

All the same, it is one more symptom of the advance of the
reign of the Holy Ghost, that not only psychoanalysis, but
the entire subject of creative energy, both in the realm of sex
as also in the world of the mind, has become so much more
prominent and has made itself so much more felt than would
have been possible before. Thanks to this increased interest
in the manifestation of creative energy in our own nature, it
may at last become possible to lift the entire subject of the
relations of the sexes into the purer atmosphere where it
belongs, and free the world from the nightmare of misunder-
stood and misapplied desire and passion, which has been and
is still the cause of such untold misery.

May the better understanding of the Holy Ghost, the great
Purifier who by the Fire of His creative Energy burns out the
dross of all that is earthly and base, help man to accomplish
that great Work of which alchemists and Rosicrucians spoke
in veiled terms, but which now can be openly discussed and
understood—the work of the transmutation of creative
energy from its physical or material manifestation to spiritual
and divine creative activity, so that the mystery of creation,
even in its manifestation as the sexual act of creation, may be
seen in its true light as a sacred and wonderful manifestation
of the presence of God the Creator in man.

Second Section

The Divine Mind

VII FROM IMAGE TO ARCHETYPE

In the previous chapters we tried to understand something of God the Holy Ghost as the creative Activity of the Divine. We must now deal with the Holy Spirit as the divine Mind. Of course, it is not possible to separate these subjects, for the Holy Spirit is One, though manifestations are many and varied. Thus the creative activity of God and the divine Mind are really one and the same, for it is the divine Mind which creates by imagination, and which calls forth the universe by thinking it. At a very much lower level, we do something similar when we create a thought form; there again it is the creative power of the Holy Ghost in us which makes it possible that our thought should become a reality. Thus we can think of the Deity as creating a universe, and as creating the forms in that universe by the power of the imagination, by making an image of them.* Just as our own thought form would disintegrate if we withdrew our attention from it, so also does the universe exist only insofar as it is maintained by that divine thought. If for a moment that divine imagination stopped, if the divine attention were withdrawn from the image, there would be no universe left.

As the universe is created and constantly re-created by the divine thought, the creative, image-making faculty of the

---

*Once again I should like to remind the reader of the paragraph in the preface, in which I explain that, in this book, I am not referring to God as the eternal, nameless reality behind all universes, but as the Logos, the Creator of a solar system.

divine Mind, so also our own individual lives are created and re-created by the power of our own thought. As we think, so we become. The creative power in our lives is not in our words or our emotions, nor even in our actions, but in the image-making power of thought. If by the creative power of the imagination we make an image of that which we aspire to be, then according to the strength of our imagination shall we be able to realize it in our daily life. This is the basis of the power of autosuggestion. Only imaginative individuals can ever be creative; without a strongly developed power of imagination no one can do great things in life.

GOD'S WORLD THE ONLY REAL WORLD

Thus the world exists because, and as long as, God thinks it, and the universe as it exists in divine thought is the only real, the only existing universe. Often people picture to themselves a perfect world existing in the divine Mind, and look upon this apparently very imperfect world surrounding us as only a partially successful attempt to follow that divine Archetype. But that is not the real relation of the world which surrounds us to the world as it exists in God's thought, of that divine Mind, which is God the Holy Ghost. There is only one real world, and that is the world as it exists in the divine thought; no other world has ever existed or can ever exist, because worlds exist only insofar as they are thought by God.

What we call the world surrounding us and what we are sometimes apt to look upon as an objective reality, existing independently of their own consciousness, is not the world at all; it is *our* world and nothing else but that. We see around us a world with a blue sky and green trees and differently shaped and colored creatures, and we believe that world to be really endowed with those qualities whether or not we are there to see them. Now this is the great illusion, the fundamental *maya* of our existence; and if we would enter the realm of the Holy Ghost, the world of the Real, we must first of all conquer this illusion, and learn to see that what we call the world existing around us is in reality nothing but the image created in our consciousness by the reaction upon that consciousness of the world as it exists in the divine thought.

OUR UNIVERSE AND THAT OF AN ANGEL

We can easily prove to ourselves the existence of this illusion, though it is not so easy to realize it fully in daily life. Let us once more state the conception which ordinary men have of the relation between themselves and the world around. They believe that that world exists just as they see, hear, taste, and smell it, that, whether they are there or not, the room in which they find themselves, the landscape which they behold, will be there in exactly the same way in which they see it now. We can easily prove to ourselves that that is not so. We human beings are endowed with a certain set of senses which react to certain groups of vibrations in air and ether, and the reaction to these comparatively limited groups of vibrations we call color, sound, and so on. In between the groups of vibrations to which we respond are enormous ranges of vibration of which we are entirely unconscious, to which we do not respond. Imagine now for a moment a being who did not respond to our particular groups of vibrations, but who on the other hand would be endowed with a set of senses responding to groups of vibrations which are practically nonexistent to us. The universe of such a being would be utterly different from our universe, and yet he would have as much right to call his universe *the* world as we should have to call ours *the* world.

We have an example of that in the difference between the perception of the world by a human being and by one who belongs to the angelic kingdom, that evolution, running parallel to our human evolution, in which we find those wonderful beings, many of whom are far beyond our normal human development, who are called Angels in the Christian religion, and Devas in the religions of India. When, for instance, we look at a living plant, it appears to us as an object with definite shape, with definite colors, and a certain sensation or hardness or softness when we touch it. But to the Angel, the outstanding characteristic of the plant would not be first and foremost its shape or color, but the life-forces flowing through it and creating and maintaining that plant from within. Similarly an electric wire through which a current is passing would appear to us as the outward shape of the wire only; yet to the consciousness of the Angel the outstanding characteristic would not be the shape of the wire, but the power flowing along it. We can easily understand that to an Angel, the appearance of the universe is very different from what it is to us. Now whose universe is *the* universe? Are we wrong, or is the Angel wrong?

We are both wrong and we are both right; either of our universes is a perfectly legitimate universe, but neither of them is really *the* universe. We both derive our universe from the Universe as it exists in the divine Mind, but the way in which it appears to us is entirely of our own making. And so we live in a world which we may imagine to be the world existing there independently of ourselves, but which in reality is our world and nothing more.

THE MYSTERY OF SENSE PERCEPTION

What we call sense perception has always been a mystery; we can read as many books on the subject as we like, but we shall never find a really satisfactory explanation of how we perceive things. We are told that in what we call sight, certain vibrations are focused through the lens of our eye, react on the retina behind the eyeball, and cause a chemical change in the rods and cones which that retina contains. After that we can trace a movement along the optical nerve to the brain center which is related to the faculty of sight, and there again a change takes place. That is the last thing we can scientifically trace of the material part of our sense perception, and then suddenly we, the conscious individual, *see* the green tree or the blue sky. Now it is evident that between this last physical manifestation, the chemical change taking place in the brain, and our consciousness, there is a gap, and that gap cannot be bridged. It does not help us in the least to trace the sense perception a few planes higher and describe the changes taking place in the astral or mental body when we see; the end is always a change in the matter of one of our bodies, and then, suddenly, in the world of our consciousness there arises that perception of the green tree. How does that image of the tree arise in our consciousness? That is the great problem which philosophy and science do not solve in a satisfactory way. Certainly, science recognizes that we are only conscious of that which exists as an image in our consciousness; it recognizes that in the last instance we do not know what is the real nature of the object outside us from which the vibration reaches our eye; and it also recognizes that the image produced in our consciousness is superimposed by us on that mysterious unknown object from which the vibration came, and that we take that image to be the original and unknown object itself. But what is not and cannot be explained for us is how the vibratory changes resulting in our body are transformed into the image arising in our consciousness, and science will never explain this until it comes to realize that it approaches the solution of this problem in the wrong way.

WHERE THE THEORY OF SENSE PERCEPTION GOES WRONG

Science begins to assume, and quite rightly so, that the world around us which we perceive by the senses is an unknown quantity, and it goes one step further and says that all we know of it is that certain vibrations of different kinds reach our senses and undergo transformations, ending in those centers of the brain matter which correspond to our various senses. After having come so far, it finds it impossible to bridge the gap between that last physical change and the image arising in our consciousness, and wonders why it cannot solve that problem. But it would be much more marvelous if it could, for it has begun to assume a duality where there is none.

Our Body and Senses Part of the World-Image Too

It is quite right to say that the universe surrounding us is an unknown quantity, but why should be single out certain parts of that universe as not unknown quantities, but as perfectly well known to us? Why say that we do not know the objects which we perceive by the senses, but that we *do* know that vibration reaches us, is transmitted through the senses, and affects certain brain centers? With regard to the problem we are considering, the vibrations reaching the senses from objects, the senses themselves, the brain, the entire body and all that belongs to it are as much an unknown quantity as those objects in the world around us which we perceive by the aid of those senses, and we have no right whatsoever to single out one group of unknown quantities, assume them to be real and known, and with them to test the remainder! How do we know that we have a brain? How do we know that we have senses? How do we know what they are like? How do we know that there are such things as vibrations? How do we know anything about chemical changes taking place? By seeing them, by touching them, by watching them through instruments devised for the purpose. That is to say we assume vibrations, senses, brain, and body to be real because we perceive them by those same vibrations, senses, brain and body; or, putting it more clearly, we test the reality of those parts of our universe by themselves.

If we are to be scientifically exact and philosophically correct, we must place all objects or creatures which we suppose to exist in the world surrounding us in exactly the same class, whether they be trees or stones, or whether they be our own senses, our body or the vibrations we can trace as coming from different objects and reaching those senses. With regard to all of them, without exception, that holds good which we found to be true with regard to the tree or any other object in the outer world: the thing itself is an unknown quantity to us, and all we know is the image produced by it in the world of our consciousness.

NOT "PERCEPTION" BUT "PROJECTION"

All, then, that we can say with regard to the world we see around us, or rather to the world we think we see around us, is this: that there is a world of the Real, the world as it exists in the divine Mind. We are there, the real we; the room in which I sit is there; the paper I hold in my hand exists there; the eye with which I think I see the paper is there, and so on—all that appears to me in my universe is there in the world of the Real, not spatially separate, but all existing in the unity of the divine Mind, and interacting, one thing on the other. When the reality in the divine world, which I call myself, undergoes the influence of other realities, as it incessantly does, the result is that in the sphere of my consciousness certain images are produced corresponding to those realities in the world of the divine Mind, and certain events take place corresponding to the interactions taking place in the world of the Real. Thus in the world of my consciousness a faithful projection takes place of the things which are interacting in the world of the Real; but the image in my consciousness, my world, is my production, my creation, a shadow thrown on the screen of my consciousness by the realities within. The images in my consciousness, which I call the world surrounding me, are thus in reality nothing else but the projection or externalization of the world of the Real, which is the only world that truly is.

THE BASIC MISTAKE

Now all this is simple enough and does not offer any serious problems. But the trouble beings when we dissociate the image produced in our consciousness from the consciousness in which it is produced—when we, as it were, take our own creations, the images in our consciousness, as things existing in themselves and quite apart from us, and then begin to wonder how we are aware of them, how we perceive that world there opposite us. Of course, we can never find the answer, because we have begun to ask the question from an entirely erroneous standpoint. The reason why the gap between the last chemical change in the brain and the image of the green tree arising in our consciousness can never be bridged, is that there is no such gap; there is not a material world entirely apart from our consciousness, which in some mysterious way produces in our consciousness those images which we call the world. What we call the vibrations reaching us from the objects—the changes, chemical or motory changes, taking place in the physical organism—are images projected in our consciousness by the interaction of the things-in-themselves in the world of the Real. They are relatively real, real insofar as there is an actual correspondence between the phenomenon which appears in the world of our consciousness and that reality which reacts on our consciousness and produces the image therein; and we are quite safe in accepting as real the conclusions of physical science, its laws and teachings, and our own daily experiences in what we call our physical world. Only we should constantly bear in mind that they are only relatively real, that is to say, they are real for and in our consciousness, insofar as they are images or "awareness" produced in that consciousness by the action upon that consciousness of things-in-themselves in the world of the Real.

PLATO'S IMAGE OF THE CAVE

We are truly like the prisoners in Plato's cave. In his *Republic* he compares men to prisoners in a cave, chained to the ground and with their faces turned toward the back wall of the cave, while behind and above them is the opening leading from the cave into the world outside. Outside the cave ordinary life goes its way, different beings pass, horses, men are moving about, but nothing of that reality is seen by the prisoners in the cave. All they see are the shadows thrown on the back wall of the cave by the real creatures and objects moving in front of the opening; and they call that play of shadows "the world."

It is the only world they know of, just as we know of no other world but that arising in our consciousness. From the shadows appearing on the wall of the cave, and from the regularly occurring appearances of the same shadows and the same shadow events, they draw certain conclusions, build up some sort of science with regard to their shadow world which to them is a very real, the only real, world. We can readily understand that they may well come to a comparatively correct knowledge of some of the realities outside the cave, may even come to know some of the laws which govern their relationships, but all the same we should call their world a very unreal one. The prisoners in the cave, however, would not believe us if we told them that their world was but a play of shadows.

From time to time one of the prisoners manages to free himself from his shackles, and discovers the opening of the cave leading to the world without. In the beginning he is dazzled by the sunlight he has never beheld and is unable to distinguish any shapes and objects, but is only conscious of freedom and all-pervading light. Gradually, however, he begins to make out the different objects in that world, and, filled with enthusiasm for his discovery of the Real after the shadowy illusions to which he has so long been confined, he returns to those who were his fellow prisoners and tells them that he has at last discovered the world of the Real, that they have always been looking at a world of shadows, but if only they will turn their faces the other way they will see a world compared to which the back of their cave is as darkness is to light, as death is to life. But none will believe him, they shrug their shoulders and pity the poor man who has become mad. They know perfectly well that their world is the real world, for they can see the shadows on the wall of the cave and these always recur in the same ways. Who is he to tell them that their world is unreal? And so they continue to play in their shadow-world, and take the unreal for the real.

WE ARE THE PRISONERS

Now that is exactly the situation in our life. We are prisoners in the cave of our consciousness, looking at the wall of it on which is projected the shadow play of the things which are in the world of the Real. We, too, are utterly oblivious of the fact that behind us is the opening to our cave, and that through it we can enter the world of Reality. And when occasionally one of our fellow prisoners has freed himself and has found the entrance to the world of the Real, and comes back and in his enthusiasm tells us of the splendors of that world, speaks to us of the hopeless insufficiency of our little play of shadows, we do not believe him, but call him mad and pity him for his temporary aberation. We say: "This world *is* real; I know that it is real; can I not throw a book on the ground, can I not hammer a nail into the wall, do I not hurt myself when I hit my finger instead of the nail, is all this not utterly and entirely real, and who is he who will tell me that all this is unreal?"

No it is impossible to explain the light to one who is blind, or the world of the Real to one who refuses to turn around and behold it. But it may help if we explain the illusion or *maya* of reality, which makes it so hard for us to abandon our little shadow world for the infinitely greater world of the Real. I would not for a moment deny that, when I hit my thumb instead of the nail I tried to hammer into the wall, or when I drop my book on the floor, something really happens, and that my consciousness of pain is quite real. But the reality of the thing, the reality of the pain, the reality of the wall, the hammer, my thumb and all my little shadow-world, is only to be found in the world of the Real. There something has happened indeed, and the different things-in-themselves in their interaction have produced a result which, in the images produced in my consciousness, I call "hammering a nail in the wall and hitting my thumb instead." The unreality is not in the event or in the things, but in the way they appear in my consciousness, my world of images, and in the importance and reality I there attach to them.

THE MEANING OF MAYA

The great *Maya* does not mean that *the* world does not exist—that would be mere madness—but it means that what I call "the world" is only the image or awareness arising in my consciousness as a result of the interaction of that consciousness of mine in the world of the Real with other realities. I then dissociate that awareness or image arising in my consciousness, place it around me in my consciousness and call it the world, the only real world. And that is the great illusion; it is the only world which is not objectively real. There is only one real world, and that is the world as it exists in the divine thought. That world is not in space and time like ours; that world has no green trees or blue sky, or any of the qualities which we possess in our world-image; but in that world there are realities, inherent in the things-in-themselves, which in our world-image we translate into terms of space and time and qualities. As long as we understand that all this entirely built up within our consciousness, we are in no danger of falling into the great illusion. But when we deny that vital connection with our consciousness and imagine that the awareness or image, the perception arising in our consciousness, is the world in itself, the real world, and if then we ask all kinds of questions with regard to the image which we have so cunningly disconnected from our consciousness, then our troubles arise, then we are gripped by *maya*. That which takes place in our consciousness is not the entrance into it of an image endowed in some mysterious way with qualities of greenness, or blueness, or hardness, or softness, but rather the projection or externalization in the sphere or our consciousness of things which are not without, but within. Thus what happens is not so much perception through the senses, as projection through the consciousness. It is only when we thoroughly realize this, that there is a possibility of our conquering the great illusion and entering the world of the Real. We have to control this idiosyncrasy of our human make-up, which causes it to project around it in the world of consciousness that which is within; and we have to focus our attention inward instead of standing lost in admiration, gazing upon our own world-image, as the prisoners in Plato's cave gaze upon the shadows on its wall.

HOW TO ENTER THE WORLD OF GOD
THE HOLY GHOST

It is possible by a certain process of meditation to withdraw our attention from that world-image in which we are so wrapped up. It is possible to stop for a moment the image-making faculty of the mind; it is possible to refuse to project outward that which in the world of the Real touches our consciousness and reacts upon it. It is possible to draw ourselves together in that point of consciousness, and through that needle's eye of consciousness to pass into the world of the Real in which that consciousness exists. For a moment there is nothing; we have withdrawn our attention from the world-image, and have not yet entered the Real, but we must not remain in that point at which the great *maya* takes place. We must push through; and, having drawn our consciousness away from its world-image and stopped its image-making faculty, we can emerge on the other side of consciousness, emerge into the world of the Real.

THE WONDER OF THE EXPERIENCE

Our first impression there is like that of the prisoner in Plato's cave who has discovered the world behind him. We are dazzled by the light of that inner world, though it is no light seen by the eyes, but a kind of inner illumination. We are conscious of an experience in which we seem to comprehend the entire world; we are aware of a rapture and an all-pervading sense of utter reality which we should never have dreamed possible. In the beginning these experiences are so overpowering that we cannot distinguish any special features of this world of the Real, but only drink in its glories, like a man who for years has been shut up in some dark dungeon and who, when set at liberty and on his return to the light and beauty of the outer world, is lost in the joy of breathing fresh air and seeing the sunlight and feeling the warmth of its rays. Gradually, however, we begin to discriminate in this Ocean of light and glory, though we must understand that it is no question of perception by the senses, by clairvoyance or anything of the kind. There are no objects in that world with shapes and colors, and there is no space, no time, as we know them here; but we experience things as part of ourselves, we are that which we know.

How is it possible in a language based on our illusionary world with its illusionary show of beauty to describe anything of the supersensual beauties of that world of the Real? How is it possible to describe beauty in which is no form, in which is no color, in which is nothing that we associate with out world-image; but in which, on the other hand, is the fullness of all that which produces our world-image? We must experience in order to know, and we can no more explain the glories of that world to those who have not experienced them than we can explain light to a blind man. No one can ever tell in words about that world, which is the world of living Truth. No book, no system, no theory, no sacred Scripture, no divine revelation even, can ever contain the truth of that world of the Real; it is esoteric because there are no words to explain it; it is hidden or "occult" because it cannot be manifest in our world of illusion. All attempt at explanation of it down here becomes a distortion, and can give only a distorted conception of that which is. All we can do is to show the way to this world of the Real, to explain that along these lines one can enter that true and real consciousness, but that every man must make the experiment for himself.

In utter loneliness the soul has to make the "flight of the alone to the Alone." None can accompany it on this journey of exploration into the world of the unknown; the soul itself alone can emerge, through its center of consciousness, from its world-image into the world of Reality. None can help; none can really tell us how to do it. All we can say is, this is the way some of us have taken; these are the things we have discovered on that way; and such are the words which very faintly express something of the glories of the world which we discovered on that journey. But every one of us for ourselves must make the journey into that terrible void of the center of consciousness, through which alone we can emerge into the world of Reality that thereafter nothing can ever shake.

It is a great and splendid thing to have knowledge of what we call science, the knowledge of our world-image. It is a still more splendid thing to have knowledge of what we term the astral and lower mental worlds; but all these are but world-images which we produce in our consciousness. It is only when we pass through the consciousness within us, and emerge on the other side into the world of the Real, that we gain a knowledge of truth and reality in which there is no illusion left. *It is then and there that we enter the world of the divine Mind, the world of the Holy Ghost.* Our own higher mind is but part of that divine Mind. We, the real being, are but a thought in that Mind, and yet in a wonderful way one with it, part of it. There is no knowledge, there is no truth but in that divine Mind; all that we sometimes would claim as our own discoveries, all our knowledge, our own intellectual achievements are but a manifestation in us of that one eternal divine Mind, the Mind of God the Holy Ghost.

THE WORLD OF
THE DIVINE MIND

When we have succeeded in withdrawing our attention from
our own world-image, when we have gathered together our
consciousness and focused it, brought it back to our center of
consciousness, turned our faces the other way as it were,
then through our center of consciousness we emerge on the
other side into the world of the Real. It is very much an
experience of turning inside-out, or perhaps we should say
outside-in. Our world-image is an exteriorization of that
which is within, and so long as we gaze on that exteriorized
image we do not come into any knowledge of the Real. When,
however, we first pass into the point from which the world-
image is projected and next, through that point, into the
reality which caused the projection in our consciousness,
then all that which in our world-image was "turned outward"
becomes "turned inward," and we ourselves seem to contain
within ourselves that which before we beheld without. Thus
it is truly a turning outside-in which is accomplished when
from the point of consciousness we emerge into the world of
the Real.

Understanding all the while that in this world of the Real
there are no spatial separations of one thing from another, we
might yet, using a simile, say that whereas in our world-image
we looked from the center of our consciousness on to the
circumference of the world-image which we had projected
around us, we now find ourselves in the world of the Real on
the circumference and center as well, in fact no phrase so
well describes this state of consciousness as that of being the

circle, the center of which is everywhere and the circumference nowhere. It is the feeling not as if one had been lost in something infinitely greater but, strange though it may sound, as if that infinite greatness were contained in one's own consciousness. The result is that when one desires to know something in the world of the Real, one focuses one's consciousness on that point within oneself which represents that particular thing, and experiences in one's own consciousness the true being of that thing.

LIFE AS SEEN FROM THE WORLD OF THE REAL

In this entering the world of the Real, the first and abiding characteristic remains the sensation of all-pervading, overpowering light, though there is no question of light which can be perceived by the senses; light is but the nearest term we can use for that which is not without, but within. With this sense of all-pervading light comes one of liberation, of the intense joy of at last being able to breathe freely, as if from the darkness of a dungeon one had come out into the glories of sunshine and natural beauty. When experiencing something of this intense reality, we can hardly understand how we could ever have taken our world seriously and imagined it to be *the* world; thinking of our world image, which in our ordinary state of consciousness we take to be *the* world, we feel a good-humored interest as that of grown-up persons watching a child at play. And yet, as soon as we are back in our ordinary state of consciousness, we, too, again play our childish game and take it very seriously indeed, but, for a while, in this world of the Real, we can appreciate things as they are.

THE REALITY OF "SPIRIT" AND "MATTER"

When next we try to lay one of the problems of our daily life beside the reality of this world, we find that that problem no longer has any meaning whatever; it is not solved, but has lost its meaning; and in its place has come the reality within. Thus with regard to a problem such as the relation of spirit to matter, we find that spirit and matter no longer have the meaning which we attach to them in our ordinary world. There we look upon spirit and matter as two opposing entities, we think there is such a thing as matter-in-itself and also a thing called spirit-in-itself. But here in the world of the Real the whole thing looks quite different; we are one with the Realtiy in which all things exist and of which all things are modes or manifestations—an ultimate atom as well as the highest being we know. There is no difference of quality between the one and the other; there is not one group of manifestations which we can call matter and the other spirit; the very words have lost their significance for us. The atom of matter when experienced in the world of the Real is as great a reality there as the highest being, though in the one there is a greater fullness of life than in the other. But there is no *essential* difference.

Now when trying to understand in this world of the Real how the idea of the difference between spirit and matter arises, we come to the conclusion, that, when a higher manifestation, or fuller manifestation, of the divine Mind comes in touch with a lesser manifestation, the lesser manifestation cannot express the greater manifestation and therefore is a limitation to it. That experience of contacting a lesser manifestation of the Divine appears in our world-image as a sensation of being limited by something which shuts us in, *which sensation we call form.* On the other hand, when we contact in the world of the Real a fuller manifestation of the divine Mind than we ourselves are, the sensation is what in our world-image we call "spirit," or "life." Thus the greater manifestation appears to the lesser manifestation as "life" or "spirit," and the lesser appears to the greater as "matter" or "form." The result of this is that one and the same manifestation can be life to a lower one, and matter or form to a higher one. Thus, for instance, we may well be life to lower manifestations, but at the same time matter to a very much loftier ones; and yet we are always the same being both in our function as life and in our function as matter. Where, then, is our great and mighty problem of the difference between spirit and matter, or life and form? What we call matter is merely the *way* in which the lesser manifestation appears to the greater. Thus spirit and matter, life and form are but terms to denote a relation between different manifestations of the divine Mind, and have in reality no meaning whatsoever in themselves. We now see that the problem as to the origin of matter and its difference from spirit is an essentially wrong problem; it can never be solved because it has no meaning. In the same way the dualities of Self and not-Self, of *Purusha* and *Prakriti,* or any of the names which we care to give them, are not distinctions between different types of things; but in exactly the same manner they are terms to denote the way in which one mode of the divine Mind appears to another; for the same thing may be Self to one and not-Self to another thing.

The moment we begin to believe in either matter or spirit, Self or not-Self, as a thing-in-itself, different in its essential nature from its opposite, we have confused the issue and raised a problem which no mind however great can solve, because the problem is wrong. Yet the reality cannot be told in words. We can try to explain how the thing appears in the world of the Real, but it is only the living experience of it which can show us, and make us feel, the utter futility of the problem and the glorious reality of the thing itself.

TIME IN THE ETERNAL

It is the same with regard to our problems of time and space. In the chapter on the dynamic universe, I have already dealt with the fact that things-in-themselves are each the entire creature from its birth as a manifested being to the very end of its manifestation as such, and that this entire being from begining to end exists as a reality in the world of the Real—in fact that that was the only real creature, and that what down here in our world-image we experience at any moment is only the non-existent cross section of that real being. Now even that term "cross section" does not really explain what it is, but be it sufficient to say that, in the world of the Real, all that down here we call time, evolution, change or growth, is present as an abiding Reality. When, living in that Reality, we consider the profound problem of the beginning of time we cannot help feeling almost amused at the problem itself, it is such an impossible question to ask; for how can a period which is a complete thing in the world of the Real have either beginning or end of a cycle of evolution, but the whole thing is a complete unity. Thus experience in the world of the Real wipes away that problem of the beginning of time, which no succession of countless *manvantaras* and *pralayas* could ever solve. The splendor of the real thing as experienced in the world of the Real is infinitely greater than any solution our intellect or logic can present and gives abiding satisfaction.

SPACE AND OMNIPRESENCE

In the same way there is no longer the problem of space in the world of the Real. Who can speak about the boundaries of space and what is beyond them, when within our own consciousness, in the world of the Real, we can concentrate on anything we desire to experience? The very possibility of separateness in space, or "size," has disappeared, and the smallest atom is as great or as small, whichever we like to call it, as the mightiest solar system. In our world-image we may see countless different creatures, all separate from us in space and distant from us, but in the world of the Real we experience them all as within ourselves. Thus groups of people, movements, nations, and races, all humanity can be experienced there as realities, which are no longer groups of different creatures put together to make a unity, but which *are* a unity, one Being bearing within itself all the multiplicity of the different creatures. It, however, impossible to put all this into intelligible language because there are no words to express the unity, in the world of the Real, of things which, in our world-image, are antinomies, always opposed and apparently irreconcilable.

IS THERE A DIVINE JUSTICE ?

We must now touch on the problems of free will and determination and that of divine Justice. To begin with the latter; the doctrine of Karma, however well it explains the causal connection of successive lives on earth, does not finally prove divine justice for the individual any more than the orthodox doctrine which looks upon every human soul as freshly created in its particular set of circumstances. When the entire future evolution of a soul is branded for good or evil by its mode of individualization from the animal kingdom, and where the poor animal certainly could not help the way in which it individualized, the problem of divine justice has merely been shifted back a few million years. This does not in any way lessen the splendor of the doctrine of Karma, but only shows that we must not call it a final solution to the problem of justice for the individual, when that problem is wrong in itself.

When we try to consider the problem of divine justice for the individual in the world of the Real, the very problem becomes absurd. The separate individual for whom we claim justice in our life here is merely a product of our world-image, and how can we desire divine justice for a separate individual when there is no such creature? In the world of the Real, we experience the totality of human experience as all belonging to one great Being and not to many separate creatures, we exult in the life of the one Being and are not in the least affected by what happens to that which, in our world-image, we call the "separate creature." Once more the problem has become meaningless, and in its stead comes the glorious reality of something which is even more than what down here we call love; a unity in which we do more than love our brother, in which we *are* that brother, in which we do not in sublime self-sacrifice declare ourselves willing to suffer in order that he may be happy, but in which his happiness and our suffering and the experience of all the countless millions of creatures are all experienced by one great Being, which we in a marvelous way become when we enter that world.

FREE WILL AND DETERMINATION

Finally we must mention the problem of free will and determination. When we enter that world of the Real there is no longer the will of the separate individual, but only the Will of the one all-embracing Being. The manifestation of that Will in what we call the "outer world" may appear to us a thing happening to us from outside, but in the world of the Real we know that it is all the manifestation of the One Will, which is our own will in the most absolute and entire sense. Freedom is absence of all limitation, and how can there be any more limitation to our will when it is *the* Will, besides which there is nothing and by which all is determined. Thus in the world of the Real determination and free will are one and the same thing.

The fact that all that can ever happen is already present in the dynamic universe of God the Holy Ghost does not in the least convey the sense of a cold and remorseless Fate which, crushing out all opposition, accomplishes its ends; on the contrary we realize that the entire future and all that can happen to us in that future exists even now in our own being, and that its appearance in our world-image, in that succession which we call time, is nothing but the manifestation of that which we already are within. Here again we err when we try to make a compromise between free will and determination, when we say that we are a little determined and a little free. In the experience of the Real we know that all that can ever happen to us "from outside," as we call it, is nothing but the expression of our own will, and that within ourselves, as we exist in the world of the Real, all that can ever happen to us is even now contained.

We could continue to describe the different way in which the problems of our world-image appear to us in the world of the Real, but these few examples may be sufficient to show how the wrong problems arising from the great illusion of our world-image are swept away in the world of the Real by That which is.

THE JOYS OF THE DIVINE MIND

There is no more exultant joy than this experience of the world of the Real. The sense of all-embracing freedom, the feeling of unlimited expansion in a Mind which is the Reality of all that we call the universe, the sense of containing all that lives, is such supreme bliss that, even if we have but experienced it once, nothing can really matter afterwards, nothing can ever shake us again. This is the greatness of the actual inner experience of the realities of the divine Mind, and no theories, no intellectual juggling, no cynicism or scepticism can ever again affect this experience in the slightest. Theosophy is the experience of the Eternal, the abiding Reality; it is the experience of the divine Mind, the experience of the world of God the Holy Ghost.

THE WAY OF THE HIGHER MIND

There are very few people who know their own mind. Though we might expect the world of our consciousness, of our own mind, to be more familiar and better known to us than the world around us, we find in practice that the opposite is true. Our attention is so much turned outward toward our own world-image, that we hardly realize that within us there is a world of consciousness very much more real than that image in which we are lost. Man has a habit of beginning to notice that which is farthest away and only finally discovering that which is near and obvious. Thus he is first struck by the wonders of the heavens above him; if astronomy is the first of sciences, psychology is the last. Thus it is only very recently that, in what is called the new psychology, science has begun to investigate the working of that wider consciousness which, to the majority of men, is still an unknown world.

When this science develops further, one of the most important departments in it will no doubt be that which deals with the workings of our mind, both with regard to the intellect, the mental instrument, as also and even more with regard to the mind itself. The result is bound to be the opening up of a new way of mental development, and that possibility we shall now consider.

First of all we must do some mental analysis and find out not only the relation between the intellect and the higher mind, but also something about the workings of both.

How We Think

What happens when we think? Thinking seems to be an activity in which all of us are engaged at least part of the day; every now and then we have to think over some problem or decide whether to do a thing or not; and yet if we were asked what we do when we thus think out a problem we should find it very hard to give an answer. We know vaguely that something happens inside and that, when someone else is thinking, we see him frown and make a very solemn face; but that is about all we know about the workings of thought. What really happens inside is the problem, and it is very difficult to analyze, for the moment we begin to watch how we think, we stop thinking. We either think and do not watch what happens, or else we watch and do not think; the difficulty is to split our consciousness so that we can think with one part and watch what we are doing with the other. It is not an easy thing to learn, but once we are able to do it the results are quite interesting, if not always flattering.

Daydreaming

The first thing we discover is that most of what we call thinking is not quite such an important and solemn work as we would make ourselves believe, and a better name for it would be daydreaming. When, for instance, we find ourselves in a bus, or just sitting in a room, lost in thought, we are in reality only daydreaming. When we watch what we are doing under such circumstances, we find that we generally build up images of ourselves in different situations and then start living and acting in those images. We hold imaginary discussions with the other *dramatis personae* in our little picture and behave in different ways with regard to them. It is quite an interesting process in its way; we are using the creative or image-making faculty of thought, and by its means creating an entire situation in which we behave in a heroic or cowardly manner as our mood of the moment may dictate. Then we suddenly wake up with a start to find ourselves sitting in a bus, or reading a book, of which all that time we were quite oblivious. If we are asked what we were doing, we say that we were thinking; but it would be truer to say that we were dreaming. Yet we must not undervalue these daydreams, because in them the current desires of our daily life are vitalized by the creative power of the imagination and set up living thought forms in ourselves which sooner or later take effect in our daily behavior. By the nature of our daydreaming we determine largely what we are to be, and that is why it is a power which we should learn to control and use for the better instead of for the worse. But we can hardly call it thinking.

THINKING OUT A PROBLEM

Let us analyze another process of thought, for instance, the solution of a scientific problem, or a problem of daily life. Now how do we set about it? First we look at the problem and state it to ourselves mentally, generally in words. These words are of course not pronounced physically, but are, as it were, said in thought; and when we watch them we find that they are only partially pronounced and form only fragmentary sentences; we take a good deal for granted in this inner conversation with ourselves! Having stated the problem, we take some particular aspect of it and, as we call it, "concentrate" on that, which really means that for a moment we exclude other subjects from our minds. Then we watch the reactions and associations which it causes in our consciousness, and if it is a scientific problem we watch whether these ramifications throw any light on the subject in question; and so step after step we work out our problem. Very often the solution does not come straight away and we have to abandon the problem for the moment. Yet the activity thus set up is not entirely stopped; the problem, as it were, simmers on quietly, even though we may not be conscious of it, and, according to the intensity of our original statement of it, as also the intensity of our desire to find a solution, a corresponding activity may be set up in the higher mind. Then, very often months or even years later, generally when we are not thinking about the subject at all, we suddenly know the solution; the thing is present in our mind.

THE FLASH OF INTUITION

It is thus, when the intellect is quiet and not specially concentrated on anything in particular, when we are in our bath or eating our breakfast perhaps, that the higher mind, our true mind, has a chance to make itself heard on any subject. We say that a solution has suddenly struck, us, and so it has; only it is not, as we often think, produced by the intellect; it is the intuitive knowledge of the higher mind which flashes into the workings of the intellect. Sometimes this happens while we are pondering over the problem, but more often while the intellect is at rest. Thus the greatest scientific discoveries or philosophical conclusions often appear while the intellect itself is disengaged. The waters of the intellect must be perfectly smooth if something of the higher mind is to be reflected therein.

NEWTON AND THE FALLING APPLE

When we come to study the history of great inventions or discoveries we find ample evidence of this. It is not likely that Newton, when he saw the apple fall from the tree, was engaged in concentrated thought on the problem which he desired to solve, but for many years he had been pondering over these problems, and the fall of the apple was the occasion when the knowledge from within could flash down into his waking consciousness. But his higher mind saw the truth of gravitation which was thus received by the intellect, the instrument of thought. In the same way, we are told that Einstein's discovery of certain elements in his theory of relativity was made when he saw a man fall from the top story of a house with a grand piano. Probably Einstein was not thinking particularly of the problem of relativity at the moment the rope gave way and man and piano came falling down; but, if true, it evidently provided the opportunity for something that his true mind knew to manifest in and through the intellect. We could multiply these instances to show how in all cases it was in the realm of the higher mind that truth was seen or experienced, and that the intellect was merely used as the instrument through which the inner vision could be interpreted.

RIGHT THEORY, WRONG PROOF

I even know of one particular case where a scientist of European fame propounded a theory which proved to be correct, but which in his publication he deduced from arguments which later on proved to be wrong. When asked how this was possible, he said: "Oh well, I knew the thing to be right, but then it needed some kind of proof!"

The proof or the logical argumentation is merely the technique by means of which the intellect makes the truth of the higher mind digestible to us, but it is not, as is so often thought, the method by which the truth is found, or even proved. Thus we sometimes find a heavy philosophical volume in which, after many hundreds of pages of argument, the philosopher brings forth the truth which, like a conjurer, he had all the time in his hat. He has seen the vision of this truth but carefully hides from us the fact that he knows what he is about to prove, and when finally the bird is produced out of the hat, he looks on with well simulated surprise at this amazing result. It would certainly simplify life if every one who wrote a book began by saying in quite simple language what he had seen or discovered in the way of truth and knew to be right, and then, if he felt so inclined, brought forth his arguments and proofs to make his conclusions more reasonable. Logic and intellectual argument are merely a technique which is entirely unproductive in itself, and by means of which anything may be proved. Thus, in philosophical discussion, it is quite easy to take two opposite views of the same question and "prove" that each of these views is the correct one. In the realm of science, such self-deception is not so easy because we have the facts of the world around us by which to test our conclusions. But, even here, we often find a theory proved, only to be superseded by the next discovery.

THE INTELLECT AN INSTRUMENT

The intellect is an instrument for the higher mind to use and nothing more; and as long as we realize its limitations in this respect it is a very useful and splendid thing. This image of the intellect as an instrument is a very useful and illuminating one. An instrument in itself is never productive; without the artist playing upon it no musical instrument can produce any results. But, on the other hand, unless the artist has the instrument to play upon, neither can he produce results. So if our intellectual instrument is deficient, if it is insufficiently developed or undernourished (for the intellect needs nourishment as well as the physical body), even the greatest inner experiences cannot express themselves down here. Thus the two are necessary; the productive and creative element is the higher mind within, and its vision of truth is the only way to knowledge; but on the delicacy of the intellectual instrument depends how far the truth of the higher mind can be made intelligible to others.

NECESSITY OF DISTINCTION BETWEEN INTELLECT AND HIGHER MIND

It is necessary that we should clearly distinguish between the higher mind and the intellect, and never attempt to use the intellect as a way to knowledge about things which belong to the higher mind. If we, as is sometimes done, drag the things of the higher mind down to the level of the intellect, the result is a distortion of truth, even though it may present itself as a beautiful logical system fitting perfectly. Above all, we must never accept the workings of the intellect as a substitute for the vision of the mind, for thus we feed on unreality. If we are to be workers, able to give living teaching and not stones instead of bread, we must know this difference between the intellect and the higher mind and gradually become familiar with this world of the higher mind which is the world of God the Holy Ghost.

IS THE MENTAL TYPE UNSPIRITUAL?

Sometimes people, who fail to distinguish between intellect and higher mind, denounce the mental type of individual as "unspiritual." Now it is quite true that in mere intellectual development there is more of danger than of advantage, and that a man who is predominantly intellectual and has not developed the higher mind has generally an entire lack of intuition and very often is emotionally arid. But, on the other hand, the development of a good intellectual instrument is necessary if we ever hope to gain an understanding of higher things. It is easy to pride ourselves on our freedom from the vices of the intellectualist when we have not developed our own intellect; but where there are no difficulties to overcome, there can be no pride in having overcome them. The man who attempts to ride a fiery and untrained horse will no doubt have very unpleasant experiences and often present but a sorry spectacle; but the man who sits astride a chair prides himself on the quietness of his steed is even more ridiculous. Thus it is not constructive to discredit the intellect; we must develop it and then learn to overcome it. The intellect is the Slayer of the real, and we are told to slay that Slayer. But first there must be something to slay.

WHEN THE INTELLECT IMPERSONATES THE MIND

The main necessity is to discriminate between the products of the intellect which are without intrinsic value and the manifestations of the higher mind which are exceedingly valuable. To the untrained mind it is very often hard to distinguish between the two. The intellect in its cunning way will present to us thoughts, doctrines, and systems which fit as nicely as a picture puzzle but which are without value except as a pastime.

The higher mind will often know things which, when translated by the intellect, may not at once be distinguishable from the workings of the intellect by those who have not learned to discriminate between the two, and thus, often, we find no distinction made between the intellect—the instrument—and the higher mind—the artist who plays upon the instrument. The result of this, in many of our discussions, is that, on the one hand, we often discredit mental work as being "merely intellectual" without discrimination, and, on the other hand, we often swallow wholesale the mere jugglings of the lower intellect which announce themselves as the workings of the higher mind. We must learn to distinguish between the two if we would enter the world of the higher mind and there learn truth.

THE DESIRE FOR KNOWLEDGE

We all desire to gain first hand knowledge about real and higher things, but often our desire is but a faint wish; many people would not mind having more knowledge, they would be quite pleased if suddenly they found themselves possessed of it, they may perhaps even wish for it in a gentle way, but they do not really desire it. It is only when the desire for truth so dominates our existence that we feel that life becomes impossible unless we gain it, that we shall find what we seek.

There is a story told of a candidate for knowledge who came to an Indian Yogi and asked him what conditions he should fulfil in order to become his disciple. The Yogi took the aspirant to a little lake near his dwelling, asked him to enter the water with him, and then held him under the surface of the water for some seconds. When the disciple came up, choking and gasping for air, the Yogi asked him what he desired most when he was under the water. "Oh," said the disciple, "I wanted air." "Well," answered the Yogi, "when you desire truth as ardently and passionately as you desired air when you were under the water, you shall find it." There are very few people who desire truth as ardently as that. They would like to know more, but they are not really unhappy on account of their lack of knowledge. As long as that is our attitude we shall not gain firsthand knowledge, we shall not enter the world of the higher mind. The first condition is an ardent desire for truth.

THE TRAINING OF THE MIND

The second condition is a clear understanding of the relation of the intellect to the mind, the instrument to the living Power within. After that our task is twofold. On the one hand, by concentration and meditation we must learn to quiet the intellectual instrument so that it becomes a docile servant of the higher mind; and, on the other hand, we must by study and reading equip the intellectual instrument with the material and the tools by means of which the Thinker can build his intellectual structure, so that he may embody the vision he has seen in the world of the mind.

But even while studying and reading we must always remember that no reading, however wide, and no study, however intense, can do more than furnish our intellect with the material necessary to make it a good and useful instrument, and that real knowledge has to come from the higher mind.

In the world of the Real all great thoughts, schools of philosophy, movements in art, and such like, exist as living realities—we might almost say living beings. There the idealism of Plato, the genius of medieval architecture, the social philosophy of Ruskin and the subtle beauty of a Shelley exist in their true and living being; and when we enter this world of the Real, we can there experience those inner things and gain infinitely more knowledge about the subject in question than any mere reading could possibly give us.

LOVE AND KNOWLEDGE

A certain way of gaining that contact with the living reality of an author's thought, or an artist's inspiration, is an intense love for that author or artist, a love so great that it unites us to him in that world of the Real, and links up our consciousness with the living inspiration of which his books or works of art are but the temporary manifestation. Thus I have sometimes found schoolboys who, in their great love for some particular author, had come to a truer and better understanding of his thought, than had learned authorities on that same author who, having read all his works, and perhaps written several volumes of commentaries, yet missed the inner meaning for lack of love for the author or for the subject. It is a profound truth that unless we have loved a book with an almost personal devotion, unless its author has been our friend and comrade while we read his books, and unless we have lived and slept with the book and treasured it as our dearest possession on earth, we do not gain that inner union which links us up to the life and thought of the author himself.

A mere dispassionate and critical study of any subject or author can never do more than give us a certain book learning, a certain grasp of a number of facts; it may enable us to quote the author abundantly, but it can never give us the living knowledge of the message he tries to bring.

A NEW WAY TO KNOWLEDGE

Thus the quickest and most certain way to real knowledge and a wide culture is the awakening of the higher mind within us, the contacting of the Holy Ghost in the world of the Real, and the experience of the living realities which there represent what down here we call schools of thought, movements of different kinds, periods of history or culture, and other subjects we may desire to know. Naturally, the outer study always remains necessary; it alone can provide the material with which the Thinker within can build a receptacle or tabernacle for the vision he gains in the world of the Real. But the mind, the Thinker himself, is the great master builder; it is his vision, his experience, his inspiration, which transforms the materials of the intellect from a chaotic mass without meaning into a noble and beautiful building.

Thus once more we say what we said in the beginning of this chapter: that it is necessary to know our own minds, necessary to know the function, the limitation and use of the intellect; but even more so to know the higher mind in the world of the divine Reality where it belongs, and through it to enter that world of the Holy Ghost, which is the world of living Truth, without which all intellectual knowledge is but as dust.

Once more we can realize the enormous importance of God the Holy Ghost in our daily lives. It is the world of the divine Mind, in which alone we can experience the living

Truth, it is in that vast ocean of inner light that we share in all that is true and beautiful and good in the wisdom and art of the ages; it is there that we gain firsthand knowledge, not by the laborious way of a mere amassing of facts, but by the direct way of touching the life of which the facts are but the outer expression.

It is by means of this direct and inner vision that we can see our entire world image, with its millions of apparently separate forms and facts and beings, coordinated and illuminated by the one living Reality of which that outer world image is but the exteriorization. We see and understand the many from the One; we see the Real through the unreal;—we have entered the world of God the Holy Ghost.

X INSPIRATION

The touch with the power of God the Holy Ghost is inspiration. The Holy Spirit really means the holy or sacred Breath, the Breath of God, the Breath of Creation by which all things are made. When this divine Breath of creative fire touches man, he is instantly galvanized into creative activity; he is inspired in some way according to his particular genius or Ray. Thus in the artist, inspiration will be the vision of the beautiful by which he creates his work of art. For the philosopher, it is the vision of truth, the illumination of the mind, in which he sees things-as-they-are and which enables him to lead humanity one step further in its discovery of the truth. In the scientist, the touch of inspiration will be that flash of intuition which makes him see the law of nature, or discover the hidden force which was indicated by his experiments and study of facts. The humanitarian, when inspired, will see the vision of a better and nobler humanity and gain the creative power to bring about some great reform for the improvement of man. In the teacher, the touch of God the Holy Ghost will cause inspired speaking, that touch of living fire which makes the spoken word a thrilling and moving power, which nothing else can ever replace. But the highest manifestation of the Holy Ghost in man is perhaps in the prophet, who, in his vision of the future, causes the light of the Eternal to shine in the world of man.

Many indeed are the manifestations of inspiration, but its essential nature is always the same; it is that touch of the creative power of the Holy Ghost which makes man more than man, which makes him God. Whatever is touched by such an inspired one is transformed into a higher and nobler thing; to talk to such a one is to be thrilled by a power which carries us with it and kindles within us a similar enthusiasm.

THE VALUE OF INSPIRATION

The "Kiss of the Muses" is a very real thing; by it man becomes for a moment the temple of the living God within, and through him the life of the world of the Real can illumine our darkness. Inspiration makes the desert of material life a wonderful garden by pouring into it the waters of living truth and beauty. Life in this world would not be worth living if it were not for those dreamers who see the vision of the Real and the beautiful, who are able to interpret it in different ways for the helping of mankind; it is by them that humanity can be moved onward and upward in its long pilgrimage; it is by them that we receive the strength to persevere, the ability to sacrifice and the power to create.

MODERN PSYCHOLOGY AND INSPIRATION

It is very curious that in modern psychology the subject of inspiration has been so neglected. Psychology has for its aim to give a theory and science of the workings of the different functions of our mind, and of the different states of consciousness we can experience. Surely the most important of these is that state of consciousness in which we touch the world of Reality, and that power of inspiration which makes us divinely creative. There is no doubt that in the near future the entire subject of the creative mind, of inspiration, enthusiasm and idealism will take a very much larger place in psychological investigation than has been the case up to now,* and the results of such a closer study for our daily life will be very great indeed.

THE TECHNIQUE OF INSPIRATION

I explained elsewhere how in the world of the higher mind things do not exist in those sectional appearances which down here, in our world-image, we call "the thing as it exists at the present moment." The present, as we have seen, has no dimension and no reality; the only real thing is the being in the world of the Real, containing within itself all that we call its past and its future. When, in touching that world of the Real, we come in contact with any such being or movement, we not only gain a vision of its future, because that future is already present in the thing-in-itself, but we also touch the creative energy, the dynamic part of it, which causes in our world-image the further evolution of the thing. It is that touch with a thing in the world of the Real which we call inspiration, and we can now understand how in inspiration we not only see a thing in its perfection or future development, but we are also fired by the creative energy to make it what it will be.

Naturally, the technique of inspiration is different in the case of the artist, philosopher, scientist, or social reformer. When the artist, in gazing upon a landscape, is inspired by the vision of its beauty and creates a great work of art, what really happens is that for a moment he has experienced the reality of that landscape as it exists in the world of the Real, and is so filled with the beauty of that reality and fired by the creative power in it, that he is able to produce an immortal work of art, whether it be a great poem, a painting, a musical composition, or a work of architecture.

It is remarkable how we never find inspiration without also finding its attendant function of galvanizing the inspired person into action. When inspired, the poet will start writing his poem, the painter will begin planning his canvas, the social reformer will begin to work out his scheme of reform, or the philosopher to express his vision of the truth in the language of the intellect, forgetful of all else, possessed by inspiration.

THE UNIQUE CHARACTER OF ARTISTIC INSPIRATION

But the special feature of art, as distinguishing it from other types of inspiration, is that in art the vision of the beautiful is embodied not merely in a combination of words, colors, sounds or forms; but that these form a living organism through which the reality, as it is in the world of the divine

Mind, can express itself, through which it can live. Thus in and through a great work of art we can at any time come in touch with the living reality that inspired it; through the work of art the door to the world of the Real is open to mankind, and the life of God the Holy Ghost can manifest itself. That is why art is the most precious of all forms of inspiration and why without it man could not live.

*Modern depth psychology has given exhaustive study to this area of human experience. Ed.

The inspiration, for instance, of the social reformer is a very different thing. He will contact the particular department of social life in which he is interested as it will be in the future, and with that vision and with the creative power that accompanies it, he can transform the world around him.

We must always remember that the vision of the Real is not the placid contemplation of a picture without, but the touch with a living reality within; and that it is always attended by this vitalizing influence which makes the truly inspired man an almost irresistible force in social life. In artistic inspiration however there is this greatest of all gifts: the embodiment of the inspiration in the organism of the work of art.

ENTHUSIASM

Inspiration is closely akin to enthusiasm. We have to go back to the days of ancient Greece to find in Greek religion, which was a religion of the Holy Spirit in its beauty aspect, a real understanding of and reverence for the ideal of enthusiasm. Now we often call a person an enthusiast when he is somewhat loud and bustling in his behavior, always full of plans, feasible or not, and always eager to make us share in them; we, then, with a good-humored smile say: "What an enthusiast he is!" But in Greece to be an enthusiast or to be "enthused" meant a tremendous thing; the priestess of the oracle in Delphi, when enthused, became filled with the divine power of Apollo. To be "enthused" meant to be filled with God.

Whereas inspiration is the contact with reality in the world of the Divine, enthusiasm in its true sense is almost a descent of the Divine into man. Thus the enthused person is for the moment God, and was revered as such in Greece, where enthusiasm was the very consummation of the religious life. Even in that civilization, there were but very few individuals who were really capable of enthusiasm; it needed a very particular type to make possible this influx of divine life. But enthusiasm was the very heart of that magnificent Greek culture, and without some understanding of it we cannot appreciate the other manifestations of the Greek genius.

IDEALISM

Both inspiration and enthusiasm are closely allied to what we call idealism. There is perhaps no term more ill-used than that word idealism, though there is also but little true understanding of inspiration and enthusiasm. When we speak of a person as "having ideals," we use that term for all kinds of different things; his ideal may be that of making much money, of gaining distinction in social life, or even of getting the better of a competitor in business. Now these are not ideals, they are simply personal plans, schemes and desires, sometimes even of a doubtful kind. Moreover, we cannot "have" ideals, no one in the world has ever "had" an ideal. We can have a table or a chair, a cat or a horse, but we cannot *have* an ideal. It is rather the other way around; the ideal has us.

When in the world of the Real we touch the idea of a thing, the greatness and creative power of it may so possess us, that we cannot do otherwise than dedicate ourselves to the service of that ideal and sacrifice to it all we have and are. It is greater than we are, and its touch is inspiration; we are willing to sacrifice for it because it is greater than we are, and because we are possessed by it—but we can never possess *it*. When we see how in great movements of social reform, or of national liberation, people will joyfully sacrifice their good name, their possessions, and even their very lives for their ideal, we can realize something of the power of idealism. To be an idealist means not only to have touched the world of the Real but also to have made that the center of our life and work; to the idealist the world of the divine Mind has become the one and only reality for which he lives, and his entire life is made subservient to that greater reality and is seen in its light. The idealist, whether fully conscious of the fact or not, is established in the world of the Real, Plato's world of Ideas, and sees what we call our world as the temporary result of that inner reality. Thus the idealist constantly pours the power of that higher and real world with all its beauties and glories into this world of outer existence, and as such he is a life bringer to humanity.

We cannot be true aspirants without also being idealists. The divine experience, is the very essence of idealism. But we must first free the word idealist from its unhappy associations with ideas of incompetence, inefficiency, and useless daydreaming. It is true that there are idealists who, seeing the vision of the Real and becoming absorbed by its beauty, lose touch with the world of daily life and become impractical and even dangerous to the community in which they live. On the other hand, we very often meet with people who have a firm grip on this outer world and are efficient and practical in their dealings with it, but who lack the vision which could make them creative. They are like blind men having the power to move but lacking the vision to see whither they should go. The impractical idealist, on the other hand, is like the man who can see the vision but who is unable to act in this world, who, with regard to this world, is to all intents and purposes paralyzed. True idealism has both vision and practical ability; the true idealist lives with his head in heaven, but has his feet firmly planted on the earth. Thus alone can he help his fellow men to see and to realize that which he himself has experienced within; thus he can become a creative power in life.

Inspiration, enthusiasm, and idealism are perhaps the noblest gifts of the Holy Ghost; by them humanity can gradually be brought to realize something more of the wonders of that world of the divine Mind which is the only real world. When, in the near future, the Holy Ghost will be more manifest and recognized than has been the case up to now, we can look forward to very much greater inspiration, enthusiasm, and idealism than we find at present. Our entire life will be transformed by that inspiring, vitalizing and creative influence of God the Holy Spirit, which is the very breath of life to a struggling humanity. Then once more shall the Holy Ghost be made manifest in man; then once again shall the world recognize that the Holy Spirit is a great and splendid Reality, and that it is to this influence that we owe the most precious things of life.

Third Section

The Mahachohan, the Representative of the Holy Ghost

THE PARACLETE AND THE MAHACHOHAN

In the early Christian Church the Holy Ghost was worshipped less as the divine creative activity than as the Paraclete or helper.

This conception of the Holy Ghost as the Paraclete is a more approachable manifestation of the Third Person than others and, when rightly understood, leads to very interesting conclusions.

The word "Paraclete" is not used for the Holy Ghost alone in the New Testament; in the First Epistle General of St. John, II: 1, he writes to his disciples: "And if any man sin, we have an Advocate (Paraclete) with the Father, Jesus Christ the Righteous." The word here translated "advocate" is the Greek *parakletos,* the past participle of the verb *parakaleo,* which means "I call to aid," or "call upon." Thus the word "paraclete" has the same derivation and meaning as the Latin *advocatus,* or advocate. *Advocare* also means to call to our aid, to call upon, and the advocate is originally the one on whom we call when we need assistance. From that meaning comes a second one which makes him not only the one whom we call, but the one who, when called upon, helps us, speaks for us, is our mediator in fact. Thus the function of this Paraclete or helper in the New Testament is to inspire those who call upon him for aid.

THE HOLY GHOST AS PARACLETE

The use of the word "Paraclete" for the Holy Ghost is to

be found in the Gospel according to St. John, XIV, XV, and XVI. It is when Christ has told his disciples that he will shortly leave them, and go to his Father, that he says: "And I will pray the Father and he shall give you another Comforter (Paraclete) that he may abide with you forever; even the Spirit of Truth whom the world cannot receive, because it seeth him not, neither knoweth him: but ye know him; for he dwelleth with you, and shall be in you." The word *parakletos* is here wrongly translated as "Comforter"; there is no justification in giving that meaning to the word Paraclete, which as we saw means "helper" or possibly "mediator". But the interesting part is that Christ here promises his disciples that when he shall have left them and will no longer be present as the One on whom they could call in their hour of need, the One who was always there to teach and help them, they shall have another One to call upon, another helper—the Spirit of Truth, who shall be in them. Thus after his departure the inspiration for their work is to come to the disciples from within.

Somewhat further, XIV: 26, he says: "But the Comforter (Paraclete) which is the Holy Ghost, whom the Father will send in My Name, he shall teach you all things, and bring all things to your remembrance, whatsoever I have said unto you." Here the Paraclete, who in the previous quotation was called the Spirit of Truth dwelling in man, is identified with the Holy Spirit with whom, in the beginning of this Gospel, John the Baptist prophesied that Christ would baptize, whereas he himself baptized but with water. Thus we here find the foundation for the worship of the Holy Ghost as the Paraclete, promised and given by Christ to his disciples.

Another interesting reference to the coming of the promised Paraclete is made in St. John, XVI: 7, where the Christ says: "Nevertheless I tell you the truth; it is expedient for you that I go away: for if I go not away the Comforter (Paraclete) will not come unto you; but if I depart, I will send him unto you." Here, in this saying of Christ, it is made very clear that the coming of the Holy Spirit to the disciples after the departure of our Lord is to give them that inspiration and strength from within, which they could not obtain as long as he was with them and they relied on him only.

In this same Chapter XVI: 13, some interesting things are said by the Christ about the work of the Paraclete: "Howbeit when he, the Spirit of Truth, is come, he will guide you into all truth: for he shall not speak of himself; but whatsoever he shall hear, that shall he speak: and he will shew you things to come." We have found that one of the gifts of the Holy Spirit is that of knowledge, not only of the past but also of the future. Here the Christ mentions among the things the coming Paraclete will do for his disicples, that he will *guide* them *into* all truth—that is to say, they will experience living Truth—and also that he will show the disciples "things to come"—that is to say, in the world of the Holy Spirit they will gain the vision of things in their true being, past as well as future.

So far, then, the foundation from New Testament sources of the doctrine of the Holy Ghost as the Paraclete. It was the Christ himself who taught his followers to call upon this new Paraclete, the Spirit of Truth; and this is what they did on that first Whitsunday, when the Holy Spirit descended upon them and within them the vision of truth was born and the gifts of the Spirit became manifest in them, which up till then they had only beheld in their Lord and Teacher. From this moment onward the Holy Spirit became a very wonderful Reality in the life of the disciples and later on in that of the early Church.

It was only later that Christians began to neglect the wonderful opportunity given to them by Christ, the opportunity to call upon the Holy Spirit at any time when they should be in need of his assistance, and it is in the hope of bringing back some realization of that tremendous privilege that the present book is written.

THE SECOND LOGOS AND THE WORLD TEACHER

In many ways the conception of the Holy Ghost as the Paraclete is a very much more approachable and individual conception of the third great Aspect of the Deity than the more abstract one of the creative activity of the Divine, the creative fire by which this universe exists. It is very much the same with regard to the Second Person of the Trinity. God the Son, the cosmic Christ, would not mean nearly so much to the Christians in their daily life if it were not for his great representative, Christ the World Teacher.

The World Teacher is One who himself is the fruit of human evolution, but who, having reached the stature of the perfect Man and become part of the great divine Hierarchy which rules this world, holds in that Hierarchy the office of World Teacher, by virture of which He not only becomes the Representative of the Second Logos, but in a very wonderful way is his Embodiment.

We can say that in a very true sense Christ is One with the Second Logos. Unity at those exalted levels is such a far more astounding reality than it can ever be down here, that it is necessarily very difficult for us to grasp how the World Teacher can, as an individual, be the product of his past human evolution, and yet at the same time One with the Second Logos. It may help us to think of the relation between the accepted pupil and his Master. The pupil not only represents the Master, but in a very wonderful way he is one with him, one with his consciousness. At a very much higher level, this is true of the relationship between the World Teacher and the Second Logos; Christ the Teacher is One with Christ the Son of God.

THE MANU AND THE MAHACHOHAN

It is not only with regard to the Second Person of the Holy Trinity that this union exists. Just as the World Teacher is a high official in the great Brotherhood of superhuman beings, and just as through him the cosmic Christ, the Son of God, becomes more accessible to man below, so also there are those in the great Brotherhood who in a similar way represent, and are One with, the First and Third Persons of the Trinity. The One who embodies the First Logos we know under the name by which he is mentioned in Hindu religious philosophy—the *Manu*. The Christian doctrine of Adam as the first man, the Father of the human race, is similar to this Hindu doctrine of the Manu, who is always in very truth the Father of the human race, and as such represents God the Father, or the First Logos.

The Third Person of the Trinity, finally, is represented in the Occult Hierarchy by One who in a similar way is himself the outcome of human evolution, and yet by virtue of his Office is not only Representative of, but in very truth One with, the Holy Spirit, or Third Logos. We know him by his Indian title of *Mahachohan* or Great Lord, and such indeed is he who holds the powers of creation and destruction of our world. In many ways, the ancient Christian conception of the Paraclete as the manifestation of the Holy Spirit corresponds with this idea of the Mahachohan, who is the Holy Spirit for this earth.

We might say that the Trinity of Father, Son, and Holy Ghost is manifest on our earth in this Trinity of the Manu, the Father of the race, the Bodhisattva or Christ, the World Teacher, and the Mahachohan who for our human evolution is the Paraclete. Above this Trinity of Great Ones for our earth there is a yet toft er one, in which the King of this world represents the Father, the Lord Buddha the Son and, again, the Mahachohan the Holy Spirit. The work done by the Three Persons of the divine Trinity for this earth is done through their representatives in the Hierarchy; They are, as it were, the agents of the greater Beings behind, and through them God's work is accomplished on earth. Thus the Manu does the work of the Father, the Bodhisattva that of the Son, and the Mahachohan that of the Holy Spirit. All forces from the three Persons of the Trinity come to our earth through their Representatives in the Brotherhood, and all forces or prayers sent up from our earth to the Persons of the Trinity ascend through the Representative Trinities just mentioned.

At present we are trying to understand something of the Third Aspect, that of God the Holy Ghost, and of the work of his great Representativen the Mahachohan.

THE WORK OF THE MAHACHOHAN AS THE DIRECTOR OF THE FORCES

In the widest sense we may say that all that we have seen in the preceding pages as the work of the Holy Spirit, insofar as it is related to our earth and the evolution taking place thereon, is done through and by the Mahachohan; He is to all intents and purposes the Holy Spirit for our earth. Thus the entire work of creation which we saw as the characteristic manifestation of God the Holy Ghost takes place through the Mahachohan; it is he who receives, controls and directs the enormous forces of cosmic creative energy which come to him from the Holy Spirit. This is only a part of his work; but when we catch a faint glimpse even of this part, we stand amazed at the tremendous responsibility it implies and the magnitude of the task.

Great and responsible as any work on earth may be, it is as nothing compared to the work of that supreme Director of the forces of whom we speak as the Mahachohan. He truly is in charge of that center of power for our earth from which comes all creative energy. In a great laboratory the misdirection of forces from the central powerhouse might cause a catastrophe or hold up the work, but in this great powerhouse of the world mistakes are impossible; the hand of this supreme Director of the forces never fails; failure here would mean destruction and death to millions. A misdirection of forces of such tremendous power to create or destroy would mean an upheaval in evolution and a world catastrophe; every force has to be directed exactly where it is needed and in the quantity in which it is needed, and anything more or less would be wrong and even dangerous. We can now realize something of the awe-inspiring responsibility placed in the hands of the Mahachohan and of the magnitude of that mind which is able to control, supervise and direct it all. To us it is entirely incomprehensible how one single Being, however lofty, can have a grasp of all the millions of different forms of creative activity taking place all the time in nature and in humanity. Yet it is the Mahachohan who, through his Creative Hierarchies, has supreme charge of that work, and more.

THE MAHACHOHAN AS THE LORD OF EVOLUTION

Then, again, the Mahachohan is the Lord of Evolution. We have seen how all that down here we call growth, change, or evolution is our perception of the divine Mind, which is the world of God the Holy Spirit, and that it is the Mahachohan who represents that world to us. Thus it is he who controls what down here we call the beginning of evolutionary movements, the introduction of new thoughts of a dynamic character and the general direction of civilization. To him truly, as it has been said, the future lies open like a book; He knows what is to come and what particular part of any cycle of evolution is to be completed at a given moment. Through the Five Rays which come under him, as their supreme Head, he controls the course of civilization and inspires the changes that take place in it.

Not only is the Mahachohan thus the Lord of creative Activity, both in nature and in humanity, but even the evolution of the individual is in his care. It is he who supervises the different steps to be taken in the evolution of the individual from his very beginning at individualization up to Adeptship. It is he who records the advancements made by those on the Path. At the present time, in view of the near return of the World Teacher, the work of the Mahachohan, as that of the entire Brotherhood, is more momentous than ever, and the opportunity given to those who are striving to serve the Brotherhood is greater than ever before. The Mahachohan watches over all who thus try to achieve the goal of evolution; and seeing His detailed knowledge of even individual pupils, we can only marvel the more at what to us appears the omniscience of this Mind.

THE MAHACHOHAN AS THE ENCOURAGER AND INSPIRER

In previous chapters we have seen how all creative effort, inspiration and enthusiasm, all idealism and all striving for purification are encouraged by God the Holy Ghost. The Mahachohan is his Representative for this earth, and all that reaches us along those lines from God the Holy Ghost reaches us through the Mahachohan. We can thus understand what a tremendous influence he is in our life, how he is not only the Lord of Creation in nature, but how our deepest and most sacred aspirations and inspirations are fostered by him. The flash of inspiration which comes to the great scientist after years of patient experimenting, revealing to him the theory or the law he tried to find; the illumination and experience of a great truth coming to the philosopher in the silence of his contemplation; the vision of beauty seen by the artist and embodied in his work; the purity of the saint and the power of the magician or priest; as also the sacred enthusiasm of the reformer—one and all are manifestations of the Holy Spirit through the Lord the Mahachohan. Truly he *is* our Paraclete, on him we can call without ever having to fear that no response may come; once we have recognized the reality of the work of the Holy Spirit and his embodiment in the Mahachohan, we know that even the smallest effort on our part calls forth a response entirely beyond our merits. When we think of the Mahachohan, we are not only filled with awe and admiration for the creative work he does, but also with a profound gratitude for the many blessings we receive from him, even though we may be ignorant of their source. The gifts of the Holy Spirit are many and varied; without them life would be but a desert; and it is from the Mahachohan, who for us is the Lord, the Giver of Life, that these gifts proceed.

What words can describe that Mind, one with the divine Mind itself, living in the supreme realities of divine thought which is the world of the Real, having in his consciousness knowledge of past and future, having in his power the control of the creative forces, for an entire world? It is only when in meditation we succeed in contacting that great Consciousness that we obtain some glimpse of the greatness of the One we call the Mahachohan.

THE APPEARANCE OF THE MAHACHOHAN

It is hardly possible to attempt any description of the appearance of the Lord the Mahachohan.

He uses an Indian body and looks a Brahmin of Brahmins, serene and dispassionate, profound of thought and of an ascetic refinement. The face is thin and clean shaven, the nose aquiline and the mouth of a silent determination. But what impresses one most of all in this wonderful face are the eyes. Looking into them we see the world; the wisdom of the ages is there, knowledge of a hoary past and of a dim, far-distant future. We feel that those eyes with one glance know our past and future and judge us, not in condemnation, but in a supremely serene knowledge of That which is. When he speaks, his words are not so much commands as the irrevocable decrees of That which is to be. His is a Countenance full of love and tenderness, but at the same time of a determination and a dispassion which will carry out the divine Plan of evolution and execute the divine Decrees, whether they mean suffering or joy to the individual. It is only such divine Love that can destroy, if necessary, out of very love for that which needs to be destroyed.

In the presence of this great Lord of Creation we feel truly as if we were in the creative center of this universe. We are silenced by the presence of such intensely concentrated force, such all powerful creative energy; the power and force we know on earth seems but he feeble play of children when compared to that force which is the one and only creative power in the universe. With the intensity of the force, a force truly cosmic in its magnitude, goes a feeling of utter control. This quiet and serene figure controls the forces of creation, the least of which has power to create or destroy beyond any conception we may have of force here on earth. One glance from him is enough to judge and to know, and at the same time to direct the creative energy necessary to fulfil the divine purpose.

There is something in the appearance of the Mahachohan which reminds us of that of the Master the Prince, though naturally His physical appearance is very different. Both suggest creative Fire and Energy. Both have a quiet and serene bearing which yet is throbbing with silent energy. Both convey the impression of world forces controlled; only the impression is even stronger in the case of the Mahachohan. His strength is as of tempered steel, flexible yet strong; his grace is that of perfectly controlled force; his countenance is one of indomitable energy and yet of supreme tenderness. Through his eyes looks the wisdom of the ages, the dispassionate look of One who knows all, who gazes upon the earth as from a mountain-top, and yet in his face and in the entire figure there is an element of joyous youth, of radiant vitality, of irresistible creative fire.

THE BLESSINGS OF THE MAHACHOHAN

Very little thought or devotion is given to the Mahachohan. There are many whose love goes out to the great World Teacher, many who realize something of the great Father of the race, the Manu; but very few to whom the Lord of the Five Rays, the Mahachohan, the supreme Director of creative energy, means anything at all. Yet even our smallest attempt to understand something more of his greatness, our humblest dedication to his great work, our very thought of love and adoration are instantly met with a response far beyond the little we can give. It is truly he who inspires new ideas and energy to carry them out, creative power to work, enthusiasm and idealism, and strength to purify and transmute our lower nature; and as we come in closer touch with this great Consciousness we receive in abundance those gifts which he, as representative and embodiment of the Holy Spirit, can bestow.

It would be well if more love and worship went out to the great representative of the Third Person on our earth, to the Lord the Mahachohan. It is his great department, that of God the Holy Ghost, which will become very much more prominent in the near future, and the more we can realize of the meaning and greatness of the Mahachohan now, the better shall we be able to assist in his great work when the time comes.

THE LORD OF
THE FIVE RAYS

The work of the three great Beings who, in the Brotherhood which governs our world, represent the divine Trinity takes place along one or other of the seven divisions of our evolution which are known in theosophical literature as the seven Rays of development.

But little is known of these seven Rays; all created things belong to one or other of them and throughout their evolution continue to develop on the same Ray. It is as if the life, as it went forth from the Divine, manifested in seven different ways which, in our evolution, have become the seven Rays of development. For our world the seven Rays correspond to the different planes on which all evolution in this world takes place. Thus what we call the first Ray corresponds to the Nirvanic plane, the world of the divine will or Atma within us, and it is usually known as the Ray of the Ruler or of the King. All things on the first Ray have some connection with this main characteristic of the Ray, and in our human evolution it is to this Ray that all politics, ruling, and organization belong.

The second Ray is connected with the Buddhic plane or the intuitional world, and it is the Ray of love and understanding, the Buddhi within us. It is the Ray of the Priest and Educator, and all that has to do with religion or education in our lives comes under this great Ray. Just as the first Ray, the Ray of the Atma or will, is representative of the First Logos, the Father, and consequently is the Ray on which the work of the Manu is done, so the second Ray represents the Second

Logos, the Son, and on it is done the work of the World Teacher, the Christ.

The third Ray in a similar manner represents the Holy Spirit and is connected with the world of the higher mind, the Manas in us. It is the Ray of creative thought, and it is along this Ray that we can come into direct touch with that world of the divine Mind which is the world of the Holy Ghost. As the Mahachohan is the Representative for our world of the Holy Spirit, this third Ray comes under His dominion and is representative of Him just as the first and second Rays are representative of the Manu and the Bodhisattva.

THE MAHACHOHAN AS THE LORD OF THE FIVE RAYS

There is, however, this difference, that the four remaining Rays also come under the direction of the Mahachohan, so that instead of there being one Ray on which his work is done, there are five Rays which are all representative of his work of creative Activity.

When once we understand how the different Rays are related to the planes on which our evolution takes place, we can see why the Mahachohan is the Lord of the five Rays and not like his great Brothers the supreme Head of only one Ray. The Rays which we have just considered are Rays which represent the divine Trinity in man; they correspond to the threefold world of the spirit, whereas the other four Rays are connected with the three worlds of illusion, the physical, emotional and lower mental worlds and, in the case of the Fourth Ray, with the center of consciousness, where the worlds within meet the worlds without. These worlds of outer manifestation are the result of the divine activity of creation of which the third Ray is representative. Thus it is from the higher mental world, with which the third Ray is connected, that the remaining worlds are most easily reached; they, as it were, come forth through that world of the divine Mind, and the four Rays connected with those worlds belong to the third Ray. This is the reason why there are five Rays of development under the direction of the Mahachohan; the divine Mind is the creative activity through which the worlds come into existence.

There is no better way to gain some understanding of the work of the Mahachohan than by studying the five Rays which come under his dominion; it is on those Rays that his work of creation takes place, differentiated in the case of each Ray according to the genius of that Ray, and the world with which it is connected. All the five Rays have as their common characteristic the work of the Holy Spirit, namely creative activity, and the distribution of creative energy to every part of the universe; and in the case of each Ray that creative work is done in the world to which that Ray corresponds. Thus the work of the Mahachohan, who is the Director of the forces for our world, is different on each of the five Rays which come under his dominion, and it is by seeing the work of the five Rays as one great work, that of the Holy Spirit for our world, that we can gain more understanding of that mighty part of the work of the Hierarchy, which is under the care of the Lord of the five Rays.

THE WORK OF THE THIRD RAY

In many ways the third Ray is most characteristic of the work of the Holy Ghost or that of His great Representative, the Mahachohan. The manifestation of the Holy Spirit in man is what we call Manas or the higher mind, and the third Ray corresponds to that principle in man as also to the higher mental world, the world of creative thought in which we are conscious of the divine Mind within us. It is along this third Ray that the approach to the world of the divine Mind, the world of the Real, or archetypal world, can be made, and in consequence the knowledge of this world is the gift of the third Ray. It is the Ray of metaphysics, of the Reality behind the outer activity; it is the Ray of living truth, the Ray on which we experience things-as-they-are, whereon we can come in touch with that abiding Reality in which the entire evolution of any creature or movement is known from beginning to end. Thus again it is on this Ray that we come to know the cyclic Law of evolution, the manifestation of the one great rhythm of creation in the many smaller and greater cycles corresponding to the *Yugas* of the Hindu philosophy. The science which traces this cyclic Law in the movements of the heavenly bodies, the science of astrology, is typical of the third Ray; by its aid we can gain that insight which shows us how all created things, even the very smallest, form part of the great cycles of creative evolution, which are manifest to us as the movements of heavenly bodies. Thus naturally astrology enables us to foretell the future by the knowledge of the cyclic Law, though it is a degradation of true astrology to make of it merely an art of fortune-telling as is so often done.

Characteristic of the third Ray is the dynamic view of the universe, in which we never see a thing, detached or by itself, but always as part of an evolutionary process. Thus every institution, movement, nation or race is understood in its relation with the past that produced it, and as the cause of the future which it will in turn produce. This view of the universe enables us to gain a far deeper understanding of any subject under consideration, because it is always seen in relation to all that produced it instead of by itself. It is the relativity of all things which is realized on the third Ray and which makes the virtues characteristic of the third Ray those of tolerance and tact.

RELATIVITY AND DHARMA

The standpoint of relativity is as yet a very uncommon one. Even in scientific literature one is constantly struck by the fact that institutions or movements are discussed and criticized by themselves, detached from that which produced them. Thus, for instance, in political science we find forms of government discussed and judged on their own merits as if such a thing could ever be, and one form will be called better in itself than some other form. Once we have gained the standpoint of the third Ray, we can see that each form of government is the natural product of a certain type of mentality reached by a nation in its evolution. Thus a form of government which expresses the point reached by some nation in its evolution is a right form, not right in itself, but right for that particular nation at that particular time. However, the same form which was right yesterday may become wrong today, and to call some forms right in themselves and some wrong in themselves is an unscientific attitude, as it fails to take into consideration the great truth of relativity.

It is this truth which is known in Hindu religious philosophy as the doctrine of *Dharma*, a word which is translated sometimes as Duty, then again as Law or Truth or even Religion. Behind all these apparently diverging translations lies one great and essential meaning—that of fitness or harmonious expression. Thus the Dharma of a nation at some particular time is the fitting expression of the life of that nation in its forms of government and social organization; and the Dharma of an individual will, in a similar way, be the harmonious expression in a scheme of life of the type and level of evolution manifest in that individual. To say that one rule of life, or one Dharma, could ever be right for the whole of mankind would be to ignore the great truth of the inequality of men, and in consequence to ignore the relation of each person's Dharma to the type he represents and to the level of evolution he has reached. Again, Dharma may mean truth, the knowledge of the true and living relations of things-as-they-are, and here also the idea of Dharma is that of seeing things in their proper relations. The result of such an outlook is tolerance.

TOLERANCE AND TACT

The intolerant man is one who looks upon all things from his standpoint and condemns all that differs from his. The tolerant man is one who understands the relativity of all things, and can see that each man's standpoint is as right for that man as his is for himself. It is the third Ray attitude of seeing things in their proper relations which gives tolerance; once we have caught a glimpse of the way in which all things are interrelated in the world of the divine Mind we can never again be intolerant. If we ourselves are idealists and take the spiritual standpoint we can yet, if we understand the relativity of things, see that the materialistic outlook is as justified for a certain type and level of evolution as our idealistic outlook is for us. We may find it necessary to oppose the materialistic outlook in the civilization in which we find

ourselves, but even in opposing it we shall know and understand why it is held by some.

Thus it is the tolerant man who is the tactful man; it is only
when we have gained that outlook, whereby we can see and
understand all things in their proper relations, that we can
meet every man upon his own path. It is this that is called
tact; tact literally means "touch"; it is the touch of the soul
which we gain by that tolerant outlook of which we spoke.
The really tactful person, when meeting someone to whom
he desires to explain anything, will first try to understand that
person's outlook on life and his particular mood of the moment, and then try to make his explanations fit in with that.
Thus, in explaining idealism to a materialist, we do not begin
by saying that all materialism is the product of ignorance and
spiritual blindness, and thus antagonize the person to whom
we speak, but we try to show him how his own materialistic
standpoint, in view of the modern theories with regard to the
nature of matter, naturally leads to idealism.

The virtue of tact as the result of the third Ray standpoint
will enable a person to grasp instantly a situation or atmosphere in which he is suddenly placed; by his inner touch with
the situation he will be able to say the right word or do the
right thing. The right word at the right time and the right thing
in the right place are manifestations of that virtue of tact
which is characteristic of the third Ray.

THE HEAD OF THE THIRD RAY

At the Head of the third Ray stands the great Chohan
whom we call the Master the Venetian. But little is known of
him, yet his work is of the utmost importance in our lives, for
he, as the Head of the third Ray, directs the creative energy
at the levels of the higher mind and his is the work of creative
thought which in our world governs evolution. The great
cyclic law of evolution, in which the millions of different
evolutionary cycles are as wheels within wheels, is his science;
astrology his magic; the vision of things-as-they-are,
His wisdom; and the unveiling of the future in prophecy, his
power. It is on his Ray that we can gain that particular vision
of things in which an entire movement, or a group of people,

is experienced as one living Being, and in which entire periods of history or evolution are known as living realities containing within themselves both past and future.

The Master the Venetian, at his exalted level, deals with what we call cultural movements as they exist in the world of the divine Mind. He directs the creative energy coming to him through the Mahachohan so as to control the starting and fostering of such movements within the different cycles and periods of evolution. Thus the culture of civilization is under his direction at the level from which he works, the world of the divine Mind.

It is not unlikely that in the near future, with the greater prominence of the Holy Ghost in this world, we shall know more of this great Chohan and his work than at the present time, but even now, though we may be unconscious of it, his mighty influence pervades our entire cultural life.

THE RAY OF BEAUTY AND HARMONY

The next Ray coming under the dominion of the Mahachohan is the fourth Ray, the Ray of Art, of Beauty and Harmony. It is this Ray which marks that meeting of the worlds within and the worlds without which takes place at the center of our consciousness. Our world of illusion, the world-image which we project in our consciousness, is threefold and we call these three worlds of illusion the physical, emotional, and lower mental worlds. When we withdraw our consciousness from these worlds of illusion and, through our center of consciousness, emerge into the world of the Real, the point or center where we make the great change is represented by the fourth Ray. It is that bridge between the world within and the world without which is sometimes called the *antah-karana,* the center of separate individuality and the point from which we can proceed inward to the world of the spirit or outward to the world of illusion. Thus we may say that the fourth Ray is not so much connected with any place or world of existence as that it represents the meeting between the world within and the world without, the focal point through which the Reality within is projected into our world image.

The work on this Ray is the direction of the creative activity, the force of the Holy Spirit, from the inner worlds to the outer worlds, and it is in this work that art plays such an important rôle. The particular function of art is not only that it embodies inspiration in outer forms; that is done also by the philosopher or social reformer who sees the vision within and expresses it in his work. But the greatness of art is that it embodies the vision in such a combination of sound, color, or whatever the artistic medium may be, that the form or embodiment becomes as a living organism through which the inner Reality can live and express itself. Thus a great work of art is a living organism ensouled by the Reality within, a channel through which the life within can manifest itself, and through which man can at all times approach the world within, the world of the Real. The artist is the one who is able to live both in the world within, where he sees the vision and gains the inspiration, and in the world without, where he embodies it in form. His life is a balance between the inner and outer worlds, and in the artistic temperament we often meet those extremes on the one hand of exaltation and rapture, and on the other hand of entire immersion in the outer world. It is only in the very great artists that that perfect harmony between the world within and the world without, which is the ideal of the Ray, is achieved.

In many ways the fourth Ray is unique. It is on this Ray alone that the mystic union of reality within and manifestation without, of "spirit" and "matter" takes place, which produces consciousness. The Birth of Horus is the result of this union of Osiris and Isis, the immortal offspring of the marriage between the inner and the outer worlds. This truly is the Ray of harmony; here heaven and earth meet and in their meeting beget the immortal creations of Art. It is the Ray of beauty; on it alone the Real appears in the world of the unreal, it is here that the life-forces of the inner world can be poured into our existence which else would be but an arid waste. Art truly is the salvation of the race, through it humanity is nourished and refreshed by the living waters of beauty.

Thus the work of the great Chohan of this Ray, the One

who is known as the Master Serapis, is connected with the direction of the creative forces from the inner worlds to our worlds of outer manifestation, and not the least of the results of that work is the creative activity of the artist.

THE RAY OF SCIENCE

The Rays which now follow are all connected with the direction and control of creative energy in the three worlds of phenomenal existence, and they are representative of the lower mental, emotional, and physical worlds.

Thus the direction of creative force and its control in connection with the lower mental world is the work of the fifth Ray and to it belongs all that we know as science. The task of science is not only the knowledge of the laws which govern this world but also the control of force by means of this knowledge. Unlike philosophy, which by the working of the higher mind travels from the contemplation of the One to the manifestation in the Many, science, characteristic as it is of the intellect or lower mine, comes to its conclusions by the observation of the Many in the world of phenomena, and then gradually classifies and unifies these many phenomena so that they become intelligible.

There is a close connection between the intellect and the higher mind; the intellect is as it were the reflection of manifestation of the higher mind in the world of illusion, and its method is exactly opposite from that of the higher mind. Yet it is when the intellect is stimulated that the flash of intuition from the higher mind can illumine it and bring the solution of a problem or the vision of a new theory, which becomes the contribution of the scientist to the world of knowledge. The method of the scientist is that of entirely accurate and exact observation of many thousands of apparently separate facts, repeating with uttermost patience and perseverance great numbers of experiments, often covering many years of work, and furnishing the material out of which his theory can be built, when the inner knowledge coordinates the outer facts. The virtue of this Ray is necessarily exactness; it is only by virtue of an accuracy of observation which seems almost incredible to the onlooker, that science can achieve its triumphs.

When we thus speak about science we must always remember that this means not only science of the physical world but science of the entire world of phenomena, that is to say, of the emotional and lower mental worlds as well. It does not make any difference that the senses used for observation in those superphysical worlds are not developed in the majority of men; the method and work is the same—accurate observation and the gathering of a number of facts, yielding the material out of which the mind can build its structure.

The work of the Chohan of this Ray, who in a previous life was the Neoplatonic writer Iamblichus, now known as the Master Hilarion, is thus partly the direction and control of creative energy by science, modern science as well as that ancient science of the unseen which by many is called magic. But, then, magic is nothing but the science of the few.

THE RAY OF DEVOTION

The sixth Ray which deals with the direction and control of creative Energy at the emotional levels is often called the Ray of Devotion. Sometimes students wonder why devotion should be a manifestation of the power of God the Holy Ghost. The manifestation of the Third Person is always of a fiery, energetic nature, and when we think of devotion we are apt to look upon it as a vague and somewhat watery emotion. This, however, is not the devotion of the sixth Ray; its characteristic is certainly devotion, but devotion of a fiery and passionate type, the entire dedication of one's whole nature to God.

On this Ray we find that great mystery of the transmutation of desire and emotion which can make man divinely creative by the spiritualization of all creative energy. In consequence, the sixth Ray is the Ray of spirituality and purity; man is truly spiritual only when his entire emotional nature has been not only controlled but transmuted, and the way of this transmutation is purity. Thus, when we come in touch with the Chohan at the Head of this Ray, the One whom we know as the Master Jesus, we find in him the embodiment of utter purity as well as of fiery devotion. His is the strength of true spirituality in which the light of the Spirit within shines through the outward man, and in which all that is of this world has been burned up by the fire of the true devotion. It is this passionate devotion, this utter control of all emotion and desire so that it becomes dedication to God, which is the characteristic of the sixth Ray, the Ray on which the force of the Holy Ghost is controlled in the world of the emotions.

THE CEREMONIAL RAY

The last Ray which comes under the Mahachohan's direction is the seventh Ray, and on it takes place the direction of the creative energy of the Holy Ghost in the physical world. This is done in many different ways, and when we come to study the work of the Chohan of this Ray, the Prince Rakoczi, we are struck by its amazing variety. Thus he is not only the Head of all ceremonial work, closely connected with the angelic Hosts, but his work is also that of international politics and the culture of the nations which come under his dominion. When once we understand that his work is the direction of creative energy on the physical plane, these apparently divergent activities can be reconciled.

Thus his work in international politics means such adjustment of the creative forces as will bring about the desired changes in the nation for which he works at the moment. For us, who so often believe in the outer world alone as real, it is hard to understand how thus, by the outpouring of creative energy, the fate of nations can be influenced, but yet it is so. Thus when, in the eighteenth century, the Master, then known under the name of the Comte de St. Germain, traveled about Europe, closely connected with influential people in the countries he visited, his work was not so much that of politics in the outer meaning of the word as that of directing the forces which determine the fate of nations by his presence in a particular country. It is for this reason that he still travels a great deal and that he uses his pupils in the countries where he needs to pour out force.

As the angelic Hosts are the agents for the distribution of creative energy to all parts of this physical world, the work of the Master the Prince is naturally closely connected with that of the Angels, both in so far as they influence nature as in their work in connection with humanity. It is, however, in ceremonial work, in ritual, that we find the closest cooperation between man and the Angelic kingdom, and it is in this work that the seventh Ray can be best understood. In ritual work we not only assist in the great work of creation by pouring out our force, small as it is, and contributing it to the divine energy, but we also bring down and distribute the forces of creation to this physical world. In ritual we create a form through which for the moment the divine powers can manifest themselves and affect this physical world, and the great lesson of all ritual is that our entire life should become a ritual, that is to say controlled action, directing force exactly where and as it is needed. Thus that ceremonial of daily life, which is expressed in courtesy and dignity of behavior, is one of the manifestations of this Ray, and one of the great qualities of its Head.

Of him, as of the Mahachohan himself, can be said that in his Presence is the fullness of life; we are thrilled by the creative energy of which he is the Channel, there is in him the strength of tempered steel and yet the grace of utter control of force.

The virture of the seventh Ray is expressed as Ordered Service; we might say that it is the perfect adjustment of creative force in this physical world by which all action, all work, is transmuted by the force of the Holy Ghost so that it becomes more than outer work, so that it becomes ordered service—the ritual of daily life.

The seventh Ray is to become the predominant Ray in the near future, just as the Middle Ages, in which devotion reached such unparalled heights, were under the domination of the sixth Ray. Thus in the coming reign of God the Holy Ghost we shall see a greater prominence of all ritual and ceremonial work, and we may also look forward to an ever-increasing conscious cooperation between humanity and the angelic hosts.

THE LORD OF THE FIVE RAYS

Thus, when we come to understand something of the work of the five Rays, which are under the dominion of the Lord the Mahachohan, we feel more then ever a profound reverence and awe for the tremendous work and responsibility in the hands of that great and impressive figure, who for our earth is the embodiment of the Holy Ghost.

Not only is he in supreme charge of the great work of creation for our earth, but in addition to that work he is the supreme Head of all that pertains to the five Rays of development we have just considered. His is the vision of truth of the philosopher, his the ideal of beauty of the artist, the patience and self-sacrifice of the scientist, his the fiery devotion of the ascetic and the splendor of the ritualist. Truly the Mahachohan is a great and mighty influence in our daily existence; there is hardly a department of our life where we do not come in touch with his work.

Through him our world is blessed by the manifold gifts of God the Holy Ghost, of whom he is the Representative in that Brotherhood which rules the world, it is through him that the creative energy is outpoured by which our world exists, by which it is maintained.

Fourth Section

The Motherhood of God

THE MOTHERHOOD OF GOD

XIII

A book dealing with the Holy Ghost, the creative Activity of God, would not be complete if it did not also consider what is sometimes called the feminine Aspect of the Deity, God the Mother, a manifestation of the Divine which in our Christian religion is often as much neglected as that of the Holy Ghost. The two are very closely connected, and we shall see how no conception of the Holy Ghost is complete which does not also consider the doctrine of the Motherhood of God.

Christianity is one of the few religions in which the feminine Aspect of the Deity is almost entirely neglected. The Holy Ghost at least is one of the three recognized Persons in the Holy Trinity, and even though the whole of Christianity might neglect this Third Person of the Holy Trinity, yet at least the Name is there, and with their lips Christians repeat that they believe in the Holy Ghost. Even though it may mean nothing to the majority, yet the mentioning of the Name alone serves as a reminder and leaves an opening for any who may have a deeper understanding of its reality to emphasize it. It is not so with regard to the Motherhood of God; this Aspect is hardly mentioned in the orthodox theology of the Church. Even insofar as the worship of Our Lady, the ever Virgin Mother, has been introduced, it has been as a comparatively late addition to the doctrines of Christianity, and excepting the Church of Rome the leading churches of the world look upon the worship of Our Lady as something extraneous to the genius of Christianity.

HINDUISM AND THE MOTHERHOOD OF GOD

Yet we only need to look back to ancient religions to see how very strongly the feminine side of the Divine has ever been brought forward. When we turn to that most ancient religion of Hinduism, we find that every male Deity has his *Shakti*, that is his feminine counterpart of aspect, and thus the idea of the Motherhood of God is interwoven through the entire structure of this great religion of Hinduism. The intense reverence for motherhood and the high ideal of woman both as the wife and as the mother, which we find in India, are very largely due to the beautiful conceptions of the feminine side of divine worship.

THE WORSHIP OF ISIS IN EGYPT

In the religion of ancient Egypt God the Mother was worshiped as Isis, the divine spouse of Osiris, and the Trinity of that great religion of light was Osiris, Isis, and Horus the Son. Now when we desire to understand what was meant by this worship of Isis, we must not be satisfied with reading learned books on Egyptology and studying the subject critically from the modern standpoint, but we must go back, as it were, into the consciousness of those ancient Egyptians, amongst whom we ourselves no doubt have lived, and try to understand what it meant to us when we invoked Isis, when we appealed to her, or when we worshiped the divine Mother. When we do succeed in experiencing that attitude of the old Egyptians toward Isis, the first thing that strikes us is how identical the conception was with that of the Great Mother in all the ancient religions. On the one hand, Isis was Nature, Nature in her productive and creative aspect, and in the worship of Isis the divine creative power working in and through nature was recognized and adored. No mortal could lift the Veil of Isis; it is only when man transcends his mortality that in divine experience he can know the meaning of Isis as the creative and productive power of Nature, great Mother Nature. Then, on the other hand, Isis meant the Ideal of tender Motherhood to the individual, she too was the

Consolatrix Afflictorum and to her the Egyptian would pray in his need, from her came that divine compassion which is the eternal attribute of motherhood. Isis was the ideal of the faithful spouse as well as that of the tender mother, not only was she faithful to Osiris, never resting till she had reassembled the parts into which he had been divided, but also she was the Great Mother, bringing up the child Horus in the midst of danger and tribulation.

KWAN-YIN, THE MOTHER OF MERCY

In the great religion of Buddhism we do not find the idea of the Motherhood of God prominent except in Chinese Buddhism, where we find the worship of the divine Mother, Kwan-Yin, inseparably bound up with the other religious worship. In trying to feel what the worship of Kwan-Yin means to the Chinese, we find the same conception of divine tenderness and compassion; Kwan-Yin truly is the Mother of Mercy, and the ideal of Motherhood and feminine tenderness she embodies is of such fragrant beauty that no words can do it justice.

DEMETER AND THE MAGNA MATER

In the religion of Greece we find many feminine Deities, but most representative of our conception of God the Mother was Demeter, the great Earth-Mother, who again is on the one side the productivity of Nature and on the other hand the Great Mother in whose protection and fostering care all lived.

In Asia Minor, during the centuries which preceded the coming of Christ, we find the cult of the "Great Mother" as the main form of religious worship, and it is interesting to notice that wherever in Asia Minor the Great Mother was worshiped, there, with the coming of Christianity, the worship of Our Lady became prominent too. Thus Ephesus, where the great temple to Artemis stood as one of the wonders of the world, became the great center of worship to Our Lady in Asia Minor, and the Church of Ephesus was dedicated to her. Then again a cave near Antioch, where Cybele was worshiped as the Great Mother, became afterwards a shrine to Our Lady, and thus, gradually, the cult of the *Magna Mater* was transformed into that of the Virgin Mary, one more proof of the similarity of the great conception of divine Motherhood present in both. Naturally, when studying the cult of the Great Mother in Asia Minor, we must not confine ourselves to some of the less desirable manifestations of it, but try to find and understand the very noble and beautiful conception which formed the true worship of the Great Mother and which gradually was transferred to Our Lady.

CHRISTIANITY AND THE VIRGIN MARY

Then finally came Christianity, which taught of the Virgin Mother who had borne the divine Child and who as such was worshiped not only as the Mother of God, but as the ideal of motherhood, the ideal Woman. We cannot be too thankful that through her the conception of the Motherhood of God was preserved in the Christian religion; the inspiration and blessing which has come to us from that divinely compassionate Being whom we call Mary, the Virgin Mother, have contributed an element of infinite tenderness, compassion and ideal womanhood to Christian thought which else would have been lacking.

There must be a very great and splendid Reality behind this universal worship of God the Mother as it has existed throughout the ages. Men do not worship unless they realize, and no worship survives unless there is a Reality behind it. Then, again, whenever we try to enter into the consciousness of the worshipers in those old religions, we always obtain the same sensation and the same idea. Thus there is no doubt about it that there is a very great truth in the idea of God the Mother and one which is essential to the life of humanity.

DANGER OF A MERELY INTELLECTUAL STATEMENT

We must, however, in attempting to understand the Motherhood of God, be very careful not to fall into a merely intellectual statement of the fact. It is easy enough to say that where there is God the Father there must also be God the Mother, since fatherhood implies motherhood, the positive implies the negative, and spirit cannot be thought of without the idea of matter. All that sounds eminently reasonable and logical, but it is no explanation at all; it is merely the restatement of the same things in different language. We are very fond of restating a problem in uncommon language and then imagining that we have solved it. Thus it would be quite easy to say that as God the Holy Ghost is the positive creative agency, so naturally there must be a negative creative agency, the feminine aspect of that which God the Holy Ghost is in the masculine aspect. That would sound quite reasonable, and I am afraid many people would accept it as an explanation, but it is nothing of the kind, it is merely a restatement of the problem in intellectual language.

We must set about it in a different way and try to experience the Reality and not be satisfied with a play of words, which is unreal.

PROBLEM OF DUALITY

When we try to understand that ever-recurring problem of duality in the world of our daily existence, the duality of spirit and matter, life and form, self and not-self, or whatever we wish to call it, we must not begin with the problem itself, because that problem emanates from our erroneous and illusionary world-image. It would be a degradation of Theosophy to present it as solving problems which are wrong. The greatness of Theosophy is not that it solves our problems of life, but that it leads us away from the world of illusion out of which the problems arise, and leads us straight into the world of the Real where we experience the divine Reality, in which the problem no longer exists.

THE EXPERIENCE OF THE MOTHERHOOD OF GOD

Thus when we come to consider the Reality of the Motherhood of God we must not begin to assume a duality of God the Father and God the Mother and then try to make a compromise between the two, linking them up somehow; that would be beginning from the wrong end. The way is to state a problem as clearly as we can and then to go into ourselves, enter the world of the Real, and see how the problem looks to us there. The result is always that we experience a Reality in which the problem no longer exists.

So it is here with regard to the question of the Motherhood of God or the feminine aspect of God the Holy Ghost. When we look at it in the world of the Real, we experience but one creative activity, not two. There is but one Fire of Creation in this universe; yet in that unity of creative activity we can see God the Holy Ghost or the eternal Mother according to the way in which we look at it. Once more there are not two different Persons or aspects, who are united in this act of creation, but it is one creative activity which, according to the standpoint of the beholder appears as God the Holy Ghost or as the eternal Mother, much in the same way as we found to be true with regard to the question of spirit and matter. We can experience that creative activity as a going-forth: the flashing creative fire of God the Holy Ghost, and we can also experience that same creative activity as being received and transmuted, when we call it the eternal Mother. The entire truth is beyond intellectual explanation altogether, but in trying to understand something of it we might use an image, imperfect though it be.

When we speak of the sunlight we think of one definite reality. Yet we can look upon that sunlight as radiating forth from the sun, and we can also look upon it as being received by the earth, warming all, causing growth, being transmuted into greater abundance and fertility. Yet it is the same sunlight in both cases. The sunlight as going forth from the sun, the radiance by which the universe lives, may be compared to the creative activity seen as God the Holy Ghost. On the other hand that same sunlight, when being received by the earth and all its countless creatures, causing all nature, all that lives, to rejoice and manifest in greater abundance, symbolizes the feminine side of creation. Thus a transformation takes place, of sunlight into growth and expansion, a transmutation into greater fullness and beauty of manifested form. Mother Earth receives the sunlight, fosters it, as it were, in herself and gives it back transformed in the abundance of fertile nature.

In a similar way one aspect of the creative activity is creative force, the other fertile productivity, but they are the same Reality looked at from a different angle. Fatherhood or Motherhood, Holy Ghost or eternal Mother, are ways of looking at and experiencing the one eternal Reality of Creation.

As we have already spoken of the Holy Ghost as the radiant or forthgoing aspect of creation, we shall now try to understand something more of the other aspect which cannot be explained better than by the term divine Motherhood.

CREATION AS THE ETERNAL MOTHER

In trying to describe the experience of it, the words which suggest themselves are tenderness, fostering care, all-embracing protection, productivity and fertility. It is a feeling as of a warm creative activity taking place, we get the feeling of being Nature itself and transmuting within ourselves the radiant powers of the creative fire into fertility of growth and abundance of beauty and form. It is a wonderful feeling, utterly different from the experience of God the Holy Ghost, and yet it is the same thing. Now we understand what was meant by the Veil of Isis and how in Isis, Demeter, the *Magna Mater* and all conceptions of the divine Mother, there were always present these ideas of Nature's fertility. Thus the reception of the creative Power, its transmutation into productivity, increase and abundance is as typical for this part of aspect of the divine Creation as the flashing forth of the creative Spark was for the Holy Ghost.

Yet it is not possible to describe at all adequately how the two, Holy Ghost and eternal Mother, are One, not a duality which somehow we manage to unite, but a Unity which we can experience in two ways. We experience God the Creator not as Father and Mother, but as One Being, Father-Mother; One Reality which can be experienced in two different ways, and which according to our experience we call Father or

Mother. The way is to withdraw into ourselves and experience the Reality, only thus can we gain any conception of this
great Mystery of Creation. Thus when we touch creation
along the line of the Holy Ghost we are thrilled by creative
power, we want to go and do things, we feel that we *can* do
things. It is the feeling of creative power and vitality, we feel
inspired to go out and create, whether it be a work of art or a
great scheme of social reform. But when we touch creation
along the line of the eternal Mother, we are aware of the
transmutation of the creative fire into that which is to be
produced, we feel as if we fostered the creative spark with the
tenderest care, so that by a process of inner transformation it
might vitalize and make productive that which before was as
dead.

There is no more beautiful expression for this feeling than
that of Motherhood; the spark of the divine fire, which was
received in that exultant joy which we know when we touch
the fire of God the Holy Ghost, is cared for and fostered
until, through all the agonies of creative work, whether it be
that of the artist, the philosopher, or the social reformer, we
produce the thing itself, give birth in the truest sense of the
word to our work, in which productivity we find a radiant joy
as of the mother for the child, very different from the joy we
knew in the moment of inspiration by God the Holy Ghost.

Thus every one of us is father-mother, but it is only when
we can be both that we can be greatly creative. In all creative
activity, whether in art or science or social work, we can
experience both the creative force or masculine aspect and
the productivity or feminine aspect, and through these we
can contact the greater Reality behind. Thus we sometimes
speak of people as having a fertile mind, and this means on
the one hand contact with the creative fire of the Holy Ghost,
the inspiration, and on the other hand with the productivity
which finally gives birth to the work or the idea itself. The
process of fermentation of creative activity is the Mother
aspect, that of inspiration the Holy Ghost aspect, and it is
only when a person is capable of both that he can become a
true creator.

THE COMING REIGN OF THE HOLY GHOST

In the near future the Third Person of the Trinity is to become more prominent in the world; the reign of the Holy Ghost is beginning. But this reign of the Holy Ghost is at the same time the reign of the eternal Mother; the Two are inseparable because they are One. This is why the Holy Ghost in early Christian literature is so often spoken of as feminine. In one of the Apocrypha the Christ speaks of "My Mother the Holy Ghost," and the idea of "Sophia," the divine Wisdom which plays such a great part in Gnostic literature, is closely connected with this feminine Holy Ghost. Thus the coming reign of the Holy Ghost is the reign both of the Holy Ghost as inspiration and of the Holy Ghost as the eternal Mother, as productivity.

This is one of the reasons why the new race unites in itself qualities which in the past were more definitely divided between the two sexes. The exclusively masculine type of man in the past, often rough in his strength, devoid of tenderness, in his worst aspect the male brute, was as much a product of this excessive separation as the exclusively feminine woman, helpless and clinging, weak and rejoicing in her weakness; as unsatisfactory a product as the merely masculine man. We must not misunderstand this, the coming type is not a type in which the differences of sex are wiped out and an equality of man and woman is attempted, in which the essential characteristics of each sex may be lost; it is a type in which the man will have lost none of his virility and strength, but will be refined by those emotions of tenderness and compassion which for a while were looked upon as exclusively the property of women; and on the other hand, woman will have lost none of her feminine characteristics, but will at the same time have gained a strength and independence which emphasize rather than destroy her womanly qualities. Thus there is a *rapprochement* between the sexes which will enable both to express more of the Holy Ghost both as the Fire of Creation and as the eternal Mother.

Before, however, we discuss more fully the changes which

the greater prominence of the Third Aspect will produce in the relation of the sexes, we must first see how it will be manifest in the coming religion.

THE COMING RELIGION OF THE THIRD PERSON

As I have already mentioned, there is at present not only a neglect of the Holy Ghost, but also of God the Mother. Now that we understand how the Two are related, we can see how that neglect of the One must always necessarily bring neglect of the Other.

Christianity has been a typically masculine religion, the idea of God the Father has so dominated the entire worship that if it had not been for the worship of Our Lady, insofar as we do find it, the feminine aspect of the Divine would have been entirely absent. It was probably necessary to have this one-sided religion, but there is no doubt that the result of it in our social life has been disastrous; causing as it has on the one hand an entirely unfounded idea of man's superiority and all the evils springing therefrom, and on the other hand the idea of woman's inferiority, bringing about a degradation of the ideal of womanhood, which could never have taken place if in our religious worship God the Mother had been as prominent as God the Father. We cannot be too thankful that in the worship of Our Lady, which by so many is looked upon as a foreign element, a later introduction into the original religion of the Christ, we find the idea of the Motherhood of God emphasized in a way so beautiful and tender that we can only wish that it had been a recognized element of our entire Christian theology.

We must try to understand fully the deep and wonderful Reality of all that Our Lady stands for in Christian worship, so that we may be able to give that worship the place belonging to it in the Christian religion, and thus bring that religion one step nearer to the ideal of the future, a religion in which the Third Person will be emphasized both as the Holy Ghost and as the eternal Mother.

OUR LADY, THE VIRGIN MARY

When we come in touch with this wonderful Being our first impression is that of an infinite tenderness, compared to which our greatest tenderness on earth looks but rough. All that can ever have been our ideal of womanhood, all that can ever have been idealized by us in our conception of Motherhood, all that we find in perfection in her. She is the Mother of all mothers, we feel in her presence that she is one who will understand all things, have compassion on all beings, and in whose tender care even the humblest and lowliest may be fostered. It is a Motherhood which embraces all living things, truly she is the Mother of all living. We know what here on earth we mean by the conception of motherhood, how the mother is the one who at all times will sacrifice herself for her child, how it is to·the mother that the child goes for comfort and protection when it is hurt or in sorrow. But there are many millions of children who never find that true motherhood, who instead of tenderness and loving care and comfort find but harsh words and cruel treatment; there is many a child who has no mother, and who cries out its sorrows in utter loneliness. Yet for all those there is a Mother greater than all earthly mothers, One who in herself is the perfection of Motherhood, whose tender care watches over every mother on earth and every child, and whose compassion and comforting love go out to all who are in sorrow and suffering. That is Our Lady, the Consolatrix Afflictorum, she who once was the Mother of Christ, who now is the Representative of God the Mother.

It is by giving the worship of Our Lady the proper place in the Christian religion, which it must have if that religion is to be complete, that we can actively assist in bringing nearer that religion of the near future, which in its ideals will show us the unity that binds what we call the masculine and feminine aspects in all things.

Thus instead of looking upon the worship of the Virgin Mary as merely a Roman Catholic and extraneous introduction into the orthodox body of the Christian Church, we must look upon it as a precious heritage, thanks to which the worship of God the Mother has not been entirely lost to the Christian religion, and which in the Christianity of the future will be a great and splendid religious ideal.

A New Relation between the Sexes

One of the greatest results of this new type of religion, in which the third aspect as the Holy Ghost and as the eternal Mother will predominate, will be a different relation between the sexes, a different conception of marriage, and an entirely changed attitude toward that great and sacred mystery of the union of man and woman by which they can be creative and produce the humanity of the future.

One of the movements leading toward a new relation between the sexes has been the emancipation of woman, and in that emancipation there naturally have been points where the movement outran its goal. But the great achievement has been this, that where even half a century ago the position of woman in social life was that of an inferior being, whose very upbringing was calculated to make her pleasing to man and a plaything for his gratification, woman has now fought free from that degrading position, in which the very gallantry shown to woman was so often but a veiled insult to the ideal of womanhood.

The Desecration of Sex in the Old Order

In the old scheme of things it was looked upon as quite natural and fitting that a young man should spend his youth "enjoying himself," having his fling and sowing his wild oats, in which "enjoyment," insofar as it did not cause an open scandal, the degradation of womanhood and desecration of the mystery of sex was not only implied but tolerated. Then often, when he had had his surfeit of pleasure and grown weary even of lust, he would consider the necessity, again dictated by custom, of settling down to a well-ordered life, taking to himself a wife, and becoming a model citizen.

Meanwhile, a girl would have been brought up on utter helplessness, with but one idea implanted in her mind: that of one day finding a husband and pleasing him. Apart from that one achievement, nothing else was considered important for her, and all her education, all her time, was spent in making her a marketable product in the marriage market. Of real life she would be kept ignorant, such ignorance being called innocence, and thus she would be brought up to a marriage, the realities and responsibilities of which she did not even understand. Then these two would be mated, the man defiled by the desecration of all that is holy in the relation of the sexes, the woman ignorant of even the very rudiments of knowledge concerning them. What else could such a marriage be but the ghastly tragedy it has been in so many millions of cases, a tragedy where the bride in all the purity of her unstained womanhood was sacrificed on the altar of a lust which had already grown weary with surfeit in the so-called "enjovments" of youth? No one will ever be able to write the history of the worldwide suffering and humiliation undergone by women thus made to serve men who often came to them ravaged by disease and unfit to be the father of their children. How can the entire history of that suffering be known where most of it has never been told, but has been undergone in utter loneliness and without any hope of sympathy or salvation from the world outside? We can only be appalled at the ghastly debt with which man is burdened until, through countless generations of an utterly different and truly spiritual attitude toward woman and marriage, he shall have wiped out the terrible guilt that now rests on his shoulders. It is incredible how, throughout those ages, man could ever have made believe to honor and reverence woman by the courtesy and gallantry shown to her in outer life, when in the things which really mattered he dishonored and desecrated the very fundamentals of womanhood and motherhood.

Motherhood a Burden or a Shame

Could it be otherwise but that motherhood itself should suffer under such circumstances? How could a woman truly respect her motherhood when it was incurred under circumstances and conditions where she was made to serve lust and desire, and where the child was begotten not for its own sake, but for the gratification of desire? It is to be marveled at all the more that under such appalling circumstances woman has continued to look upon motherhood in as noble a way as she has done, that she has carried so willingly the great burden of the bearing and rearing of children with the incessant self-sacrifice entailed in it.

Yet the ideal of motherhood has suffered. Many women nowadays, in their misunderstanding of the emancipation of woman, think that for woman to be free of the slavery in which she found herself before, means that she is no longer to be first the mother of the race, but that first of all she is to make her way in business or in any of the professions, which now are open to her. Then again there are many who, by the unworthy conception of marriage in which they have been brought up and into which they have been forced, do not reverence their own motherhood as they would if their marriage were really the union it should be, and whose one idea is to be bothered by their children as little as possible.

Finally, there is the legion of those whose motherhood is not sanctified by the bond of marriage, who have been made tools of the lusts of men and are henceforth outcast and condemned by the same men who made them what they are. That not only these millions of victims should suffer the ignominy of being unmarried mothers and thus come to look upon their motherhood as a sinful burden, but that even the children born of such connections should be branded as illegitimate by a society which suffers the wrong conditions which made their birth possible, is a mark of shame, branded so deeply on the face of our times that it will take ages to efface.

The union of man and woman in the act of creation is the most sacred gift bestowed upon humanity by God the Holy Ghost and the eternal Mother. It is the one act in which man approaches the Divine, in which he himself can create. Until that most sacred mystery of our human life is raised from the mire of lust into the pure air of a consecration by love, there is no hope of a better humanity; a race begotten and born in lust can never be a race of noble and dedicated men and women. We can but marvel that the present race is as good as it is when we see the conditions under which it is brought into existence.

THE NEW COMRADESHIP OF THE SEXES

Fortunately there are and have always been exceptions, those true marriages where the relation between man and woman is natural and noble, where the act of creation is hallowed by love, and where motherhood has been surrounded by all the care and tenderness, all the reverence and awe of which it is worthy.

In the future that shall be the ideal; the new religious ideal of God the Creator, who is both the fire of creative activity and also the eternal Mother, will transmute the relations of the sexes and all that belongs to it in our individual and social life.

Thus in the new race which is even now being born among us, man and woman shall be equals insofar as they stand side by side as comrades in the pilgrimage of life, meeting in the independence of their own individuality, yet each representative of the ideal of his or her own sex. Thus more and not less of true manhood shall be manifest in man, and more and not less of true womanhood in woman, even though in each there shall be a deeper understanding of and response to the other sex. In social life both men and women shall have their parts, not that women will try to do the work for which man is better fitted, but that each sex will contribute that element in the social life of a nation and a race which it alone can bring.

THE SACREDNESS OF SEX

The marriage of the future will thus be the meeting and mating of two free souls, each of whom comes to this union in true love, and woman will have the same right to exact the purity in man which so often he now dares to exact from her, denying it by his own past. Then the act of union, which creates the new body, will be looked upon in the light of a divine Mystery, the great act of consummation of that union which we call marriage. The teaching of the coming religion about God the Creator, both as the Holy Ghost and as the eternal Woman, and the understanding of the great Mystery of cosmic Creation will ennoble and spiritualize the act of union between man and woman which is the symbol of it. Thus this union will be transmuted into an act of love, which shall be as a prayer to the soul for whom thus in a noble love an earthly tabernacle is being prepared. Only thus can bodies be created for a coming race pure and refined enough to be temples for the Divinity that dwells in all men.

THE IDEAL OF MOTHERHOOD

What a different conception of motherhood such relation-ship would bring! Instead of being forced to look upon motherhood sometimes as a shame, often as a burden, motherhood would be the glorification of womanhood, that highest service of woman to the race, of which she alone is capable, and the period of pregnancy in which the new body is gradually being prepared for its great purpose would be surrounded by that beauty and inner preparation which it needs.

What greater and more potent help, what more inspiring ideal can there be in this reverence of motherhood than that of the Great Mother, Mary the ever Virgin Mother? It does not matter whether we know her, the ideal of Motherhood, by that name or by any of the other names under which she is worshiped in religions other than the Christian, as long as it is the same great Reality which is recognized. Man will reverence the eternal Woman in the woman he loves, the Great Mother in the mother of his child, and by the ideal of Motherhood, embodied in that great Being whom we of the Christian religion call Our Lady, all motherhood shall be ennobled, the world transformed.

THE WORLD OF GOD THE CREATOR

Thus when we come to know God the Holy Ghost and God the Mother as Realities of our daily life, our entire world is transformed.

The contact with God the Holy Ghost, who is the Fire of Creation and the Divine Mind lifts us out of the confusion and darkness of our ordinary life into the light and clearness of that world of the Real in which we experience things-as-they-are. It is as if we had been in a valley where in the darkness of dense woods and jungles, not able to see the sky above us, not able to see the landscape around us, we had struggled on for many ages, making our way up the mountainside step by step, through innumerable difficulties. Then comes the moment when at last the ground is clear, and in the full blaze and glory of the sunlight we reach the mountaintop from which, in clear and unimpeded view, we can look down on the entire world. Now we can see that dark valley through which we struggled for so long, we can see how from all sides approach to the mountain is possible, and how men err and wander about by not being able to see the vision of the mountaintop. Is there a joy more intense and thrilling than that of thus experiencing the glories of the divine Mind, of living, be it but for a moment, in the freedom, the light and the all-embracing unity of that Mind in which the universe e-xists? Yet such joy, such supersensual beauty is the part of those who touch the world of God the Holy Ghost. In that touch we are kindled by that divine Breath, which is the living fire of inspiration, our entire being glows with a celestial fire which is the creative power of the universe, we are illumi-nated by the light of inner Wisdom, bathed in the glory of that divine Mind, and thus we stand, gazing upon a world, radiant with the beauty, vibrant with the love of God the Holy Ghost.

And in the experience of the eternal Mother, which is but another way of experiencing God the Creator, we enter into that all-embracing Motherhood in which the creative fire is fostered, tenderly cared for until it can become productive in the abundance and beauty of living form. In that experience is a tenderness and compassion, a protective warmth, in which the great Mystery of cosmic Creation is everlastingly contained.

Just as in the divine Mind we saw the world as it is in God the Holy Ghost, so in the divine Mother we see the veil of Nature lifted and the marvel of universal Creation becomes known to us as that eternal sacrifice by which the world is maintained.

Can there be a greater gift to mankind than this better understanding of the Third Person of the divine Trinity, God the Creator, the divine Mind and the divine Mother? Let us then try to understand and experience those wonderful Realities so that we may worship the Holy Ghost and the eternal Mother in our daily lives, so that within us may take place that divine transmutation of the creative energy, that *Magnum Opus* by which man becomes more than man, by which man becomes God. Then the day will come when we ourselves, having transcended our humanity and claimed the Divinity of which now we are oblivious, shall be one with God the Creator, when we shall consciously join in the great Hymn of Creation, and when through us that eternal Mystery shall be accomplished which is the work of God the Holy Ghost, the Creator, the Lord, the Giver of Life.